CONTENTS

Editor's Introduction: *The Context of This Issue*
F. GERALD KLINE 7

Introduction: *Some Proposals for Continuing Research on Youth and the Mass Media*
PETER CLARKE 11

Parental Influences on Adolescent Media Use
STEVEN H. CHAFFEE
JACK M. McLEOD
CHARLES K. ATKIN 21

Adolescents, Creativity, and Media: *An Exploratory Study*
SERENA E. WADE 39

Children's Response to Entertainment: *Effects of Co-Orientation on Information-Seeking*
PETER CLARKE 51

Sociological Approaches to the Pop Music Phenomenon
PAUL M. HIRSCH 69

Top Songs in the Sixties: *A Content Analysis of Popular Lyrics*
RICHARD R. COLE 87

Pop Music in an English Secondary School System
ROGER L. BROWN
MICHAEL O'LEARY 99

Family and Media Influences on Adolescent Consumer Learning
SCOTT WARD
DANIEL WACKMAN 113

About the Authors 127

SAGE CONTEMPORARY SOCIAL SCIENCE ISSUES 5

MASS COMMUNICATIONS AND YOUTH: SOME CURRENT PERSPECTIVES

Edited by

F. Gerald Kline

and

Peter Clarke

SAGE PUBLICATIONS *Beverly Hills / London*

PUBLISHER'S NOTE

The material in this publication originally appeared as a special issue of AMERICAN BEHAVIORAL SCIENTIST (Volume 14, Number 3, January/February 1971). The Publisher would like to acknowledge the assistance of the two special issue editors, F. Gerald Kline and Peter Clarke, in making this edition possible.

For information address:

SAGE PUBLICATIONS, INC.
275 South Beverly Drive
Beverly Hills, California 90212

SAGE PUBLICATIONS LTD
St George's House / 44 Hatton Garden
London EC1N 8ER

Printed in the United States of America

International Standard Book Number 0-8039-0335-9

Library of Congress Catalog Card No. 73-89939

FIRST PRINTING (this edition)

MASS COMMUNICATIONS AND YOUTH:

SOME CURRENT PERSPECTIVES

The Context of This Issue

F. GERALD KLINE
University of Michigan

When this project was originally conceived, we decided to focus our attention on research that was being done in a variety of cultures. It seemed necessary to examine the distinctive differences that associate with mass media presentations as well as youth groups in diverse cultural settings if we were to offset the narrowness of empirical and theoretical focus that accrues with studies done in only a "Western" setting—in particular, the American setting. There was also a strong concern for assembling the articles for this issue around research that derived from a concern for theory-building. Much of the media research has been descriptive, emphasizing prediction and showing little or no concern for explanation. Needless to say, as one can see from scanning the list of authors and their institutional affiliations, we did not succeed in our goal of making this an issue of comparative research. We think we have done a better job in finding relevant research that has a theoretical focus or has the potential for moving in that direction.

There are reasons for the problems that we found in trying to reach our goals. Although there is much research being done in the area of the mass media, little devotes itself exclusively to youth use. Despite the sudden surge of interest in the effects of violence in the media, we found that this is an area which has had little sustained empirical research. Major work by

Schramm et al. (1961); Himmelweit et al. (1958); and Maccoby (1951, 1954) has had only sporadic follow-up. And this has been the case to an even greater degree in areas outside of Britain and the United States.

Another problem which has beset us in attempting to reach our goal is the way in which mass communication research has evolved. As my coeditor points out, much of the work has been done in sociology and psychology, with concern for integrating the findings into the more general aspects of those fields. Studies done within the narrower confines of "mass communication research" have only recently started to encompass a broader social science approach. Thus on the one hand we have findings that are relevant but separate from a comprehensive theoretical approach, and on the other, findings that are interesting but possibly spurious given the narrowness of view. The articles presented here make an attempt at moving toward a middle ground.

In 1970 I attended the International Sociological Association meetings in Varna, Bulgaria, to make contact with those researchers from different parts of the world who have a common interest in youth and the mass media. It was a frustrating set of meetings from a number of perspectives. Ideologically there were great differences which prevented a true dialogue from taking place. Secondly, the amount and kind of research being undertaken was reminiscent of past experiences in some of the Western countries with a strong empirical tradition. One common characteristic, however, was a concern with what youth *ought* to be doing and what kind of media presentations were *best* for them. There was a ring of inevitability here which, in all probability, added to my frustrations.

Needless to say, though, the developments of the last decade in all parts of the world have accelerated interest in the area we have chosen to deal with in this issue. The massive growth in media technology and, to some observers, the concomitant growth in youth rebellion have produced a sense of urgency that one can easily discern in countries of differing ideological persuasion.

We hope this issue will spur a renewal of interest in this area for the social science disciplines. Socialization as it relates to the development of mass media use patterns; the reciprocal effect of mass media use in overall socialization; exploration of why certain media preferences exist at differing points in the adolescent life cycle; behavioral outcomes as a consequence of media use either separately or in conjunction with other informational inputs; and institutional responses to the pursuit of certain kinds of content are only a few areas that can benefit from further research. If we are to have a better understanding of how the mass media operate in the overall social context, it behooves us to examine it in the developmental process that is youth.

REFERENCES

SCHRAMM, W., J. LYLE, and E. PARKER (1961) Television in the Lives of Our Children. Palo Alto: Stanford Univ. Press.

HIMMELWEIT, H., A. OPPENHEIM, and P. VINCE (1958) Television and the Child. London: Oxford Univ. Press.

MACCOBY, E. (1954) "Why do children watch television." Public Opinion Q. 18 (Fall): 232-244.

--- (1951) "Television: its impact on school children." Public Opinion Q. 15 (Fall): 421-444.

Introduction

Some Proposals for Continuing Research on Youth and the Mass Media

PETER CLARKE
University of Michigan

Most contributors to this issue on "Mass Communication and Youth" share a loose intellectual bias. It is that mass communication behavior has social origins and social consequences. The most fruitful way toward an understanding of the importance of mass communication to young people is to look at how communication fits into a context of social relationships, perceptions, and expectations.

Chaffee, McLeod, and Atkin explore how adolescents' mass media behavior relates to patterns of communication socialized within the family. These patterns are mapped along two dimensions—a socio-orientation, in which children are urged to avoid disagreements in discussions with others; and a concept-orientation, in which controversy is permitted and even sought.

Wade organizes her study of teenagers' media behavior around the concept of creativity, an individual trait, but quickly branches into social characteristics. These include the extent to which creativity, as opposed to intelligence, leads youngsters to integrate media materials into social relationships. Wade also is concerned with the effects of family environment on linkages between creativity and mass media behavior.

Clarke advances a general model for examining social implications of mass communication and applies it to a study of adolescents' information-seeking about an entertainment experience—attendance at symphony concerts. The model provides a framework within which one can study how mass communication facilitates social comparisons among persons.

Brown deals directly with how teenagers' absorption into the pop music culture is a function of friendship ties, and how a reputation for knowledge of hit tunes depends on popularity among peers and actual knowledge of what is currently on the hit list. His study, conducted in English schools, goes on to examine the social class and academic characteristics of pop music fans.

Hirsch does not analyze social correlates of listening to popular music, but his paper, nonetheless, recognizes social processes that have produced the pop music industry. Cole brings us up to date about the verbal content of popular songs, although, as Hirsch points out, we should avoid assumptions about how this content is perceived by the audience or how the content is diffused in the audience's network of social relations.

Ward and Wackman are concerned with family communication in a specialized but prominent area of behavior—product purchasing. Their analysis probes relationships between children's use of the mass media and their attempts to influence family consumer decisions.

The research reported here should be viewed against the backdrop of prior sociological inquiry into mass communication. In the evolution of communication research, there have been conspicuous efforts to encourage study of relationships between mass media behavior and the many social affiliations and processes that characterize the audience. As early as 1935, Cantril and Allport (1935: 259-267) presented an elaborate inventory of how the mass media could facilitate social behavior and provide feelings of kinship.

Studies stimulated by the discovery of opinion leaders have often suggested how exposure to a mass medium may be contingent on social opportunities for using its content (Katz and Lazarsfeld, 1955; Katz, 1957). Unfortunately, these studies sometimes have been unclear about whether "leaders" were dispensing information or influence, or whether the messages exchanged between persons had their origins in the media (for exceptions to this latter criticism, see DeFleur and Larsen, 1958; Shibutani, 1966; Troldahl, 1966).

Another tack has been study of media use as collective behavior—joint listening to music, watching television, or attending movies (Maccoby, 1951; Freidson, 1953; Johnstone, 1961; Clarke, 1963). The type of media content often incorporated into subsequent social relationships has been explored by the Rileys (1951), by Bogart (1955), and by Wilensky (1964).

Katz and Foulkes (1962) surveyed some of the social adjustment consequences of collective media use and media-based social interaction.

Instruction by the media in social behavior has been another frequent topic of research (Herzog, 1944; Forer, 1955; Gerson, 1966; Clarke and Esposito, 1966), although many investigations in this area have been limited to content analyses without corresponding attention to audience behavior (Hayakawa, 1957; Horton, 1957; Gieber, 1960; Brown, 1961; Carey, 1969).

Research reviews also have played a part in keeping alive sociological perspectives in mass communication research. Ennis (1961) presented a potpourri of ways in which group properties and relational variables could spice studies of media behavior. His essay, written when some observers (Berelson, 1959) were advertising a wake for communication research, was primarily hortatory. The Rileys' chapter (1959) covered some of the same research. Larsen (1964) updated the field with a review that mainly dealt with effects of the media on attitude formation and change.

Research on the diffusion of innovations (Rogers, 1962, 1969; Coleman et al., 1966) has perhaps done the most to perpetuate our awareness of how mass communication behavior is mediated by group processes. Contributions from this work to communication theory have probably been reduced, though, by the eclecticism of many workers in the field. The pattern of current studies is to predict the adoption of innovations by combining a grab bag of variables in a linear regression formula. When predictors come from areas as diverse as economics, personality, communication, and community norms, distinctive contributions from the mass media to social processes are more likely to be obscured than revealed.

Finally, a contrasting body of communication research has examined media use as substitutive behavior—compensating for a lack of rewarding human ties rather than facilitating social integration. A variety of approaches can be illustrated. Olsen (1960) analyzed aggregate census data and movie gate receipts to show that high per capita attendance at films is associated with high rates of population mobility. Presumably, migration between and even within cities is associated with low rates of group membership and socializing outside the family.

Maccoby (1954) has reported that middle-class children whose parents are severe in punishing aggressive tendencies and lack of obedience spend more time with television than children of parents who make fewer behavior demands. McLeod et al. (1965) have tested correlations, with mixed results, between several indices of media use and a measure of alienation that includes expressions of normlessness, personal isolation, and the ineffectiveness of concerted action.

Few of the studies just mentioned dealt specifically with teenagers and their communication behavior. Yet the study of youth and the mass media seems an especially important place to concern ourselves with the social correlates of communication. Young people are increasingly thought of as a community, if not a subculture. The peer group is a recognized anchor point in the formation of youngsters' social values.

A number of study areas await exploration. For example, how are children socialized by peers, family, and school into adopting patterns of media consumption? The paper by Chaffee, McLeod, and Atkin in this volume reviews some of the evidence, often gathered within the rubric of modeling theory. At least two developments complicate further research on this question: (1) the rapidity with which new communication opportunities are becoming available to Western youth, and (2) the possibility that parents and teachers are socialized by children as often as the reverse. A flux in communication technology and a breakdown in traditional authority are compelling justifications for longitudinal studies of media socialization.

Another question to be explored is under what circumstances the mass media are used as guidelines for standards of behavior? There is a strong, widespread suspicion that hairstyles and clothing are mass-communicated via the personae of rock stars and other entertainment heroes. Can these same individuals be enlisted successfully in the fight against social problems, such as drug abuse?

Part of the answer may be found in learning how mass-communicated "advice" interacts with perceptions of one's own social milieu and the conditions under which youngsters identify with distant, rather than proximate role models (Zajonc, 1954; Maccoby and Wilson, 1957).

And a third question for study is whether children's reputations among their peers are derived from their use of mass communication channels? Brown's study of record-listening provides a case in point, but involvement with the teen culture surely extends beyond knowledge of the Top 10. Girls' knowledge of fashions (from magazines?) and boys' savvy about hot-rodding (from magazines or newspapers?) are two additional information bases that could contribute to peer status.

Which base works for a teenager probably depends on characteristics of his social system, as Coleman's (1961) clever analysis suggests. If the base differs between social systems, the kinds of mass media behavior that are instrumental for gaining status are sure to differ too. Here is another reason for incorporating social variables into studies of adolescent communication behavior.

There are some cautions, however, to suggest in the way we define mass communication in future research. When we ask young people about their use of television, newspapers, magazines, books, and other media, three factors are commonly confused in the resulting data. These are the availability of specific media channels, the content preferences of our respondents, and their decoding preferences.

The first factor, availability, has received some attention in studies of cognitive selectivity in information-seeking (Sears and Freedman, 1967). Robinson (1969) seems to be one of the few researchers in the area of leisure and communication to recognize the possibility that much media behavior represents "wallpaper experience"—a convenient way to kill time until something more interesting comes along. To some adolescents, reading magazines may fill the gap between getting home from school and dinnertime. The publications parents buy are stacked on the coffee table, and our indices of media use faithfully record these children as fans of adult fare like *Time* or *McCalls.*

Also temporal availability is important for persons unwilling to adjust daily routines to take advantage of broadcast schedules. Electronic videotape recording devices or the expanded schedules of cable systems may someday change this, but the dynamics of television use have been shown to be particularly sensitive to competing activities and their time displacement (Samuelson et al., 1963).

These environmental influences on a person's access to communication vehicles require us to take pains to distinguish between purposive use of the media and exposure to the media out of a sense of lassitude. Each kind of mass communication behavior is interesting—but for different reasons and in different research contexts.

The second matter, content preferences, is troublesome too, since many communication studies seek to make inferences about content gratifications on the basis of channel use. For example, Schramm et al. (1961) distinguished between children who were "reality-" or "fantasy-oriented" by noting the extent to which they were absorbed by print media versus television. Of course, each of these channels offers the user a variety of content from which he can extract several gratifications. Furthermore, persons may expose themselves to a medium with only a hazy idea of what they will encounter. This is particularly the case with movies, where there are social and investment constraints against leaving a disappointing film. The act of attending *Alice's Restaurant* or the number of hours spent viewing television are poor indicators of the entertainment values one seeks to satisfy.

The direct measurement of content preferences in the media (Clarke, 1968a, 1968b) is only a partial solution. Sometimes, categories of content, which persons are asked to judge for appeal, represent the researcher's system of discriminating among media offerings (for examples of researcher category systems, see Bush, 1960; Steiner, 1963). Other times, studies have not inquired into respondents' familiarity with media content, such as individual television programs, before obtaining preference ratings. As a result, a low rating may mean rejection of the program or ignorance about it.

The third factor, decoding preferences, is almost totally unresearched. Some youngsters may enjoy television because it engages two sense modalities and is undemanding. Others may avoid books because of modest reading skills.

Solutions to these conceptual problems in children's mass communication behavior are not easy. One approach is to start by studying adolescents' interest in finding out about things like fashions, rock musicians, science, and drugs and then focusing on how they search the environment for this information. This approach holds questions of channel use (like frequency of reading a magazine) in abeyance while first determining what categories of information are salient to youngsters. An illustrative series of survey questions might go like this:

(1) Is there anything about fashions or styles in clothing that has interested you lately? What is it?

(2) Where did you first find out about that? Did you find out more about it any other way?

(3) Is there anything else you would like to find out about it?

(4) Where do you think you could find that out?

Of course, the topic of fashions is replaceable. The questions are meant to measure purposive communication and to identify the mass media experiences that lead to reducing adolescents' uncertainty about things that interest them. At the same time, we learn about youngsters' reliance on interpersonal sources.

We can discover more about their role as information givers by adding questions like the following:

> Did you talk to anyone else about it and tell him something he did not already know? Whom did you talk with? What did you tell him?

Much of the social fabric in communicative acts emerges directly from this line of questioning. For example, the items can be used to identify adolescents in terms of the ratio of their information-seeking to information-giving about topics. "Dead ends" in communication networks are persons who find out about issues but do not pass on information. "Broadcasters" are those who dispense a great deal of information in relation to the amount they seek. These communication types, and others, should be located in the adolescent social structure before one turns to questions of interpersonal influence or persuadability.

Other details of teenagers' social environment must be obtained from additional questioning about such characteristics as gregariousness—their range of acquaintanceships—and integration into family and friendship networks (see Erbe, 1962).

Of course, information-seeking is not the only reason for viewing, reading, and listening to the media. The presence of other rewards can be noted by comparing data about purposive use of communication channels with data from more typical survey questions about favorite television programs, amount of magazine reading, record-listening, and the like. It is doubtful, however, that the *nature* of media gratifications is susceptible to direct survey questions. Rather, our research designs will have to express alternative gratifications in terms of audience characteristics that can be correlated with communication behavior.

Studies of the socialization of media use have at least one additional step to take—that of determining how youngsters perceive others' orientations toward topics and media sources. For example, in order to conclude that parents socialize children's media search about politics and government, we would want to find some similarity between children's behavior in this realm and their images of mothers' or fathers' communication behavior. This similarity may be contingent on children's general aspirations to be like one of their parents (Clarke, 1969).

The potential among adolescents for accepting mass-communicated standards of behavior can be estimated by learning where they turn to find out about dating, dress, and similar topics about which they are uncertain and relating this to developmental changes in behavior. Again, longitudinal research designs are desirable.

The reputational outcomes of using the mass media can be charted by quizzing youngsters about information-seeking and information-giving on topics valued in peer and family social systems. The extent to which use of particular media channels leads to reputational status can be determined if studies encompass an entire social system, like an age stratum at school.

These few illustrations do not exhaust the questions that could be raised about the social relevance of adolescent experiences with the mass media. Our aims in gathering the papers in this issue are to provide a report of work in progress and to stimulate theory-building in this area. Our contacts with researchers in North America, Europe, and Japan convince us of a lively international interest in the role communication plays in the transition young people are making toward a postindustrial society.

REFERENCES

BERELSON, B. (1959) "The state of communication research." Public Opinion Q. 23 (Spring): 1-6.

BOGART, L. (1955) "Adult talk about newspaper comics." Amer. J. of Sociology 61 (July): 26-30.

BROWN, H. (1961) "Self-portrait: the teen-type magazine." Annals 338 (November): 13-21.

BUSH, C. R. (1960) "A system of categories for general news content." Journalism Q. 37 (Spring): 206-210.

CANTRIL, H. and G. W. ALLPORT (1935) The Psychology of Radio. New York: Harper & Row.

CAREY, J. T. (1969) "Changing courtship patterns in the popular song." Amer. J. of Sociology 74 (May): 720-731.

CLARKE, P. (1969) "Identification with father and father-son similarities in reading behavior." Presented to the annual convention, Association for Education in Journalism, Berkeley, California.

--- (1968a) "Does teen news attract boys to newspapers?" Journalism Q. 45 (Spring): 7-13.

--- (1968b) "Reading interests and use of the print media by teenagers." Report to the American Newspaper Publishers Association Foundation. (mimeo)

--- (1963) "An experiment to increase the audience for educational television." Ph.D. dissertation. University of Minnesota.

--- and V. ESPOSITO (1966) "A study of occupational advice for women in magazines." Journalism Q. 43 (Autumn): 477-485.

COLEMAN, J. S. (1961) The Adolescent Society. New York: Free Press.

--- E. KATZ, and H. MENZEL (1966) Medical Innovation. Indianapolis: Bobbs-Merrill.

DeFLEUR, M. F. and O. N. LARSEN (1958) The Flow of Information. New York: Harper & Row.

ENNIS, P. H. (1961) "The social structure of communication systems: a theoretical proposal." Studies in Public Communication 3 (Summer): 120-144.

ERBE, W. (1962) "Gregariousness, group membership, and the flow of information." Amer. J. of Sociology 67 (March): 502-516.

FORER, R. (1955) "The impact of a radio program on adolescents." Public Opinion Q. 19 (Summer): 184-194.

FREIDSON, E. (1953) "The relation of the social situation of contact to the media in mass communication." Public Opinion Q. 17 (Summer): 230-238.

GERSON, W. M. (1966) "Mass media socialization behavior: Negro-white differences." Social Forces 45 (September): 40-50.

GIEBER, W. (1960) "The 'lovelorn' columnist and her social role." Journalism Q. 37 (Autumn): 499-514.

HAYAKAWA, S. I. (1957) "Popular songs vs. the facts of life," pp. 393-403 in B. Rosenberg and D. M. White (eds.) Mass Culture. Glencoe: Free Press.

HERZOG, H. (1944) "What do we really know about daytime serial listeners?" in P. F. Lazarsfeld and F. N. Stanton (eds.) Radio Research, 1942-1943. New York: Duell, Sloan & Pearce.

HORTON, D. (1957) "The dialogue of courtship in popular songs." Amer. J. of Sociology 62 (May): 569-578.

JOHNSTONE, J. W. C. (1961) "Social structure and patterns of mass media consumption." Ph.D. dissertation. University of Chicago.

KATZ, E. (1957) "The two-step flow of communication: an up-to-date report on an hypothesis." Public Opinion Q. 21 (Spring): 61-78.

--- and D. FOULKES (1962) "On the use of the mass media as 'escape': clarification of a concept." Public Opinion Q. 26 (Fall): 377-388.

KATZ, E. and P. F. LAZARSFELD (1955) Personal Influence. Glencoe: Free Press.

LARSEN, O. N. (1964) "Social effects of mass communication," pp. 348-381 in R. E. L. Faris (ed.) Handbook of Modern Sociology. Chicago: Rand McNally.

MACCOBY, E. (1954) "Why do children watch television?" Public Opinion Q. 18 (Fall): 239-244.

--- (1951) "Television: its impact on school children." Public Opinion Q. 15 (Fall): 421-444.

--- and W. C. WILSON (1957) "Identification and observational learning from films." J. of Abnormal and Social Psychology 55 (July): 76-87.

McLEOD, J., S. WARD, and K. TANCILL (1965) "Alienation and uses of the mass media." Public Opinion Q. 29 (Winter): 583-594.

OLSEN, M. E. (1960) "Motion picture attendance and social isolation." Soc. Q. 1 (April): 107-117.

RILEY, M. W. and J. W. RILEY, Jr. (1959) "Mass communication and the social system," pp. 537-578 in R. K. Merton, L. Broom, and L. S. Cottrell, Jr. (eds.) Sociology Today. New York: Basic Books.

--- (1951) "A sociological approach to communications research." Public Opinion Q. 15 (Fall): 444-460.

ROBINSON, J. P. (1969) "Television and leisure time: yesterday, today, and (maybe) tomorrow." Public Opinion Q. 33 (Summer): 210-222.

ROGERS, E. M. (1969) Modernization among Peasants: The Impact of Communication. New York: Holt, Rinehart & Winston.

--- (1962) Diffusion of Innovations. New York: Free Press.

SAMUELSON, M., R. F. CARTER, and L. RUGGELS (1963) "Education, available time, and use of mass media." Journalism Q. 40 (Autumn): 491-496.

SCHRAMM, W., J. LYLE, and E. B. PARKER (1961) Television in the Lives of Our Children. Stanford: Stanford Univ. Press.

SEARS, D. O. and J. L. FREEDMAN (1967) "Selective exposure to information: a critical review." Public Opinion Q. 31 (Summer): 194-213.

SHIBUTANI, T. (1966) Improvised News: A Sociological Study of Rumor. Indianapolis: Bobbs-Merrill.

STEINER, G. A. (1963) The People Look at Television. New York: Alfred A. Knopf.

TROLDAHL, V. C. (1966) "A field test of a modified 'two-step flow of communication' model." Public Opinion Q. 30 (Winter): 609-623.

WILENSKY, H. L. (1964) "Mass society and mass culture: interdependence or independence?" Amer. Soc. Rev. 29 (April): 173-197.

ZAJONC, R. (1954) "Some effects of the 'space' serials." Public Opinion Q. 18 (Winter): 367-374.

Parental Influences On Adolescent Media Use

STEVEN H. CHAFFEE, JACK M. McLEOD
University of Wisconsin (Madison)

CHARLES K. ATKIN
Michigan State University

The developing child in modern society is typically introduced to the mass media in the home, and it is at home that he is most likely to use several varieties of print and broadcast media. By the time he reaches adolescence, it is plausible to assume that his patterns of media use have been shaped by social influences in the home, particularly his parents. Many parents express concern about mass media influences on their youngsters and appear to be quite willing to modify their own behavior if it will encourage desirable patterns of media use by their adolescents.

THE DATA

In this paper, we will present data from a recent field study of some 1,300 families, in an examination of the influence of parents, and of the

---

Authors' Note: *The major support for the research reported here is a grant to the first two authors from the National Science Foundation (GS-1874). Other sources of support for portions of the research include the University of Wisconsin Graduate School, the National Institute of Mental*

structure of parent-child relations, on the uses the developing adolescent makes of the mass media. This survey was conducted in 1968 in five eastern Wisconsin cities and involved an interview with one parent plus two questionnaires completed by a child from each family, at various points in time. The cities were selected to provide a wide range of socioeconomic and political milieus; they ranged in population (1960 census) from about 17,000 to nearly 70,000. Details of the study design have been reported elsewhere (Chaffee, Ward, and Tipton, 1970); here we will describe only those measures and procedures that are pertinent to this report.

The paper is divided into two main parts. In the first, we examine the degree to which the adolescent's media habits resemble those of his parents, and we consider several possible explanations for the similarities that are found. As will be seen, the similarities are not strong and are at least as amenable to alternate interpretations as they are to the inference that parents directly influence adolescent media use. In the second part, we take a more sophisticated approach by looking for indirect influences based on the structure of communicatory relationships between parent and adolescent. This Family Communication Patterns factor has been shown to relate to a variety of political and communicatory variables in a series of preliminary studies (McLeod et al., 1966; Chaffee et al., 1966; McLeod et al., 1967).

While we take a decidedly sociological approach to the question of parental *influence,* it should be noted that nonsocial methods of parental *control* can affect the adolescent's media use as well. Many families have rules and quotas governing what the youngster may watch on television, listen to, or read. Greenberg and Dominick (1968) found that more than one-third of a sample of urban adolescents felt that their parents had "the most say-so" about the TV programs the family would view. Hess and Goldman (1962) report similar results from a survey of mothers of grade-school children. And, while few U.S. homes lack a television set, parents can effectively curtail their youngsters' reading by, for example, *not* subscribing to magazines that do not interest them.

Health, and a grant to the University of Wisconsin Computing Center from the National Science Foundation. The studies have been conducted in the Mass Communications Research Center of the School of Journalism at the University of Wisconsin.

But in this paper we are concerned with social factors in the home beyond these immediate economic and power relationships. The patterns of interest and motivation toward communication that the youth will carry into adulthood are, we assume, those that he has learned socially, rather than those that are simply imposed on him so long as he remains at home. The parent who exercises direct control over his youngster's media consumption may not have as much influence over that adolescent's later media habits as does the parent from whom the child learns general patterns of communication.

As a working assumption, we will look for sources of parental influence specifically in the *communicatory* behavior of the parent. We will examine direct effects based on the parent's own use of the mass media and then some indirect effects based on his interpersonal interaction with the youngster.

DIRECT INFLUENCES OF PARENTAL MEDIA USE

Modest but consistently positive correlations between adolescents and their parents have been found in a number of studies for types of media use that commonly occur at home. In two major early studies of television and children, the authors concluded that these statistical associations were due to "parental example" as a direct influence on the youngster (Himmelweit et al., 1958; Schramm et al., 1961). This interpretation is sometimes called "modeling," on the assumption that the child observes the parent's behavior and, in an attempt to behave in a more adult manner, models his media use after the parent's. In Schramm's rather strong words, "example is the best persuader" and exercises "a very potent kind of influence" over a youngster's viewing. This implies that the youngster will watch programs his parents watch and, conversely, will refrain from viewing what his parents do not (Schramm et al., 1961: 182). These two processes can be considered separate hypotheses, which we will call *positive modeling* and *negative modeling.* (The concept of negative modeling should not be confused with the process by which a rebellious youngster might consciously avoid behaving the way his parents do–a pattern that might be called *antimodeling.)*

More recent researchers have expressed strong doubts about the generality of the modeling hypotheses after reviewing extensive evidence on parent-adolescent similarities in reading (Clarke, 1969a, 1969b) and television viewing (Chaffee, McLeod, and Atkin, 1970). One obvious alternative explanation that they suggest might be called *reverse modeling*; i.e., it could as well be that the child's media use influences the parent's, rather than vice versa.

Several studies provide direct reports of reverse modeling. For example, Clarke (1963) asked parents about their favorite program during a specific viewing evening. Regardless of the type of program cited–adventure, light entertainment, public affairs, or sports–about four out of ten parents said that their adolescent child had selected or recommended the broadcast. In a study of high school seniors, Bottorff (1970) reported more instances of parents asking program advice from adolescents than vice versa. Without trying to estimate precisely how often reverse modeling occurs, we can reasonably assume that it is not such a rare event that it can be ignored as a substantive hypothesis.

But these statistical similarities could easily exist without any social influence in either direction. One factor that could account for some of the correlations is *opportunity*; for example, when one person in the home is watching television, others may be unable to avoid exposure to the program that is on. Probably a more serious challenge to any modeling inference is the likelihood that parent and adolescent are independently led to use the mass media in similar ways by other factors which on persons in the same family are identical or nearly so–socioeconomic status, residential locale, intelligence, physical capacity, family conflict or tension, and so forth. Factors such as these have often proven to be useful predictors of individual television use (Schramm et al., 1961).

Even with these several kinds of potential factors, the patterns of parent-adolescent similarity are spotty. Clarke (1969a) finds no relationship in the amount of book-reading by boys as compared with either parent. He does find correlations for some kinds of magazines (e.g., news and general content) but not for others (e.g., sports and outdoors). Closer examination of the father-son relationship (Clarke, 1969b) shows a stronger correlation when the son identifies strongly with his father. But in television program preferences, we find that sons resemble thier mothers more than their fathers (see below).

Several other pieces of evidence cast doubt on the modeling hypotheses. One is that the parent-adolescent correlations are often weaker among older adolescents–indicating that the youngsters' media behavior is *not* gradually shaped into an approximation of adult patterns in the home. Another is the simple fact that adolescents spend far more time watching television than their parents, and yet the strongest parent-child correlations are found in the case of television use (Chaffee, McLeod, and Atkin, 1970).

TABLE 1
PARENT-CHILD MEDIA USE CORRELATIONS, BY GRADE LEVEL

Media Use Index		Parent's TV Time	Parent's TV Entertainment	Parent's TV News	Parent's News Reading
Adolescent's TV Time	Jr.Hi	**.16**	.15	-.04	-.11
	Sr.Hi	**.20**	.07	.03	-.11
Adolescent's TV Entertainment	Jr.Hi	.00	**.11**	-.02	-.04
	Sr.Hi	.12	**.07**	.00	-.05
Adolescent's TV News	Jr.Hi	.05	.06	**.13**	.09
	Sr.Hi	.00	-.01	**.13**	.07
Adolescent's News Reading	Jr.Hi	-.01	.02	.10	**.09**
	Sr.Hi	-.04	.00	.05	**.06**

NOTE: Cell entries are Pearson *r*s, and differ from zero at the following significance levels:
$r \geqslant .08$, $p < .05$
$r > .10$, $p < .01$
$r \geqslant .13$, $p < .001$

Table 1 summarizes the correlations in our study between four indices of parental media use and four comparable measures for the adolescent in the same family. For the youngster, the data are composites of responses to two self-administered questionnaires, which were given out at school in May and November of 1968. The parent indices are taken from at-home interviews in September-October by the staff of the Wisconsin Survey Research Laboratory. The adolescents were not told of the parent interviews; parental permission for the November adolescent questionnaires was requested at the end of each parent interview. Either the mother or the father was interviewed, with the selection of the parent systematically alternated according to a fixed schedule.

The TV Time measures refer to the person's self-estimate of the number of hours he spends watching television per day. For the parent, this is a single-item measure, referring to "an average weekday . . . in the evening after 5 p.m." For the adolescent, that item was combined with a question (asked six months earlier) referring to "yesterday."

For both parents and adolescents, the TV Entertainment index is a three-item sum based on the frequency with which they report viewing comedies, westerns, and adventure or spy shows.

TV News for the parents is a three-item sum based on the frequency of viewing national news broadcasts, news specials, and interview shows. For the child, a more elaborate index was constructed by adding to that measure some additional items on viewing 1968 election campaign programs.

News Reading indices were constructed separately for parents and adolescents based, in both cases, on a variety of measures of newspaper and magazine reading plus interest in public affairs material.

As Table 1 shows, the correlations (in bold type, on the diagonal) between parent and adolescent are not large for any of these measures, although most are significantly nonzero because of the large Ns. The highest figure in Table 1 is the modeling correlation for TV Time, a variable on which similarity could easily be due to simple opportunity to view rather than to social influence. Somewhat smaller correlations are found for viewing of TV Entertainment and TV News, respectively. These too could be inflated by opportunity. For News Reading, the correlations are of borderline significance; reading, of course, is an essentially private behavior, and one on which opportunity factors would have relatively little positive effect. (The negative factor of the lack of family subscriptions to periodicals, however, can still create a specific opportunity effect on reading of particular materials.)

Table 1 can be grouped into four quadrants of measures, if it is assumed that TV Time and TV Entertainment form one closely related pair and that TV News and News Reading form a second. Inspection of the correlations between different measures in Table 1 (i.e., those correlations that are not boldface) indicates that this is a valid assumption. Within these two pairings, the average nonboldface correlation is $r = .08$ ($p < .05$). In the upper right and lower left quadrants, by contrast, none of the correlations across categories is as high as .07 and the mean is $r = -.02$. This can be interpreted to mean that any modeling influences between parent and child are specific as to content, but nonspecific as to medium. That is, the parent's general (entertainment) television use is associated with the youngster's general television use, but not with his specific attention to television news; the reverse modeling pattern is the same. Further, the attention to news by the parent, regardless of the medium (television or print), is associated with attention to news (via either medium) by the adolescent.

Particularly strong *negative* correlations are shown in Table 1, between parent's News Reading and adolescent's TV Time; indeed, the data are stronger than are the positive parent-child correlations for News Reading. Although such data are far from conclusive, this suggests that the parents may influence their youngsters more by what they *do not* do than by what they do–i.e., that their modeling influence could be primarily a negative one. If the parent reads news materials a great deal, the adolescent is somewhat more likely to either read or watch news presentations but is definitely less likely to devote much time to television (other than news programming).

It is difficult to accept the conclusion that heavy parental viewing is positively modeled by the youngster, although the parent-child TV Time correlations are the strongest in Table 1. The TV Time correlation becomes somewhat stronger from junior to senior high school–but in this period the adolescent markedly reduces his total viewing time, on the average. Conversely, three of the four correlations for News (TV and Reading) decline with age–while the adolescent is typically increasing his news consumption and approaching adult levels. The positive statistical association for TV Time, then, might more reasonably be attributed either to negative modeling (children whose parents do not view gradually come to view less) or to reverse modeling.

Separate analyses by sex of parent and of adolescent showed stronger correlations with the mother, *regardless of the youngster's sex.* It is difficult to imagine a positive modeling process in which a teenage boy patterns his behavior after his mother's more than his father's. This mother-child association was true at both grade levels.

In all, then, our data give rather little support to the notion that parental example in media use provides an important model for the adolescent, except perhaps in a negative fashion. The statistical relationships are weak, they are not specific to a given medium, and they do not explain the general developmental trends for media use during adolescence.

In another survey, we were able to test the viability of the opportunity hypothesis, as an alternative to the various modeling inferences (Chaffee, McLeod, and Atkin, 1970). A sample of 225 sixth- and ninth-grade youngsters and their mothers in one small Wisconsin community was about equally divided between homes with one television set and homes with more than one set. We reasoned that the opportunity for two persons in the same home to be viewing the same program (without any interpersonal influence) would be greater in the one-set homes. Where a second set is available, the mothers and their children could more easily select different programs. But the mother-child correlations were as large, on the whole, in the two-set homes as in the one-set across a wide variety of programs. Apparently the second set functions more to provide privacy and convenience than to resolve program-selection differences. The kinds of programs viewed by mothers (e.g., news) tend to be broadcast in different time slots from those preferred by adolescents (e.g., situation comedies and adventure-drama programs), so there is perhaps not much chance for opportunity factors to "force" viewing even in one-set homes. The adolescents report viewing with siblings much more often than with parents; indeed, they view alone as often as with parents. There is at best some oblique support for an opportunity hypothesis in our finding of higher parent-adolescent correlations when we ask about specific programs than when we ask about general types of programs (Chaffee, McLeod, and Atkin, 1970), but this difference could easily be due to greater reliability of measurement for specific questions. The opportunity effect has yet to be clearly demonstrated empirically; it might be more likely to be a major factor where younger children are involved.

It certainly cannot be inferred that adolescent modeling of parental media use *never* occurs. In a Maryland survey, about half the adolescents in the sample said they sometimes happen to watch TV programs just because their parents are watching (Chaffee, McLeod, and Atkin, 1970); this suggests a combination of opportunity and positive modeling. In that same survey, however, two-thirds said they thought their parents sometimes watched programs just because they (the teenagers) happened to be watching them (reverse modeling plus opportunity). So our general inference would be that positive modeling is only one factor, and a lesser one at that, among many that contribute to parent-child media use similarities. And, since the correlations representing these similarities are rather low, modeling by adolescents appears to be a very minor factor indeed.

As we have seen, adolescents differ considerably from their parents in media use. But they also differ widely from one another, and one can assume that these individual differences grow out of background experiences that are more pervasive than simply observing the use their parents make of the mass media. In the next section of this paper, we examine the structure of habitual parent-child communication as a socializing influence that can account for media use differences among adolescents. We will return later to the modeling correlations and consider them in light of the effects of family communication patterns.

INDIRECT INFLUENCE OF FAMILY COMMUNICATION

Our typology of families, based on patterns of parent-child communication, has been developed in a series of studies in various demographic settings (e.g., McLeod et al., 1967; McLeod et al., 1968-1969). We rather consistently have found that there are two general dimensions of communication structure on which families vary and that these dimensions (which we had originally thought of as polar opposites) are positively correlated only to a very slight extent. We have assumed (with considerable support from various pieces of data) that these communication patterns help guide the child in his "cognitive mapping" of situations he encounters outside the immediate family context, e.g., at school, in relation to public affairs issues, and mass media use (Chaffee et al., 1966). We also have some evidence that the influence of family communication, as generalized to other situations, persists well into adulthood; it appears to become part of the developing individual's "personality" that he carries outside the home (McLeod et al., 1967).

Table 2 shows the dimensions of this typology, the names we have given to its four family types, and the relative incidence of each type in our junior and senior high school samples.

The first kind of relation, which may be pressed on a very young child, is called "socio-oriented." In families that stress this socio-orientation, the child is encouraged to maintain harmonious personal relations, avoid controversy, and repress his feelings on extrapersonal topics. The parent and the adolescent were asked separately about a number of kinds of interaction with one another that would encourage this orientation in the

TABLE 2
FAMILY COMMUNICATION PATTERN TYPOLOGY, BY GRADE LEVEL

	Low Socio-Orientation		High Socio-Orientation		Row Total
	"Laissez faire"		"Protective"		
Low Concept-Orientation	Jr. Hi:	25.1%	Jr. Hi:	22.6%	47.7%
	Sr. Hi:	28.3%	Sr. Hi:	20.2%	48.5%
	"Pluralistic"		"Consensual"		
High Concept-Orientation	Jr. Hi:	21.5%	Jr. Hi:	30.8%	52.3%
	Sr. Hi:	27.5%	Sr. Hi:	24.0%	51.5%
Column Total	Jr. Hi:	46.6%	Jr. Hi:	53.4%	100.0%
	Sr. Hi:	55.8%	Sr. Hi:	44.2%	100.0%

NOTE: Percentage figures indicate the proportion of the total sample within the grade-level cohort that falls in each family communication category. For the Junior High cohort, n = 641; for Senior High, n = 650.

youngster; these scores were summed to provide a single index for each parent-child pair. Some typical items:

(1) (Parent) urges (child) to give in on arguments rather than risk antagonizing others.

(2) (Parent) answers (child's) arguments by saying something like, "You'll know better when you grow up."

(3) (Parent) lets (child) know that (child) should not show anger in a group.

(4) (Parent) stresses that there are some things in life that are either right or wrong.

(5) (Parent) says that the best way to stay out of trouble is to keep away from it.

(6) (Parent) says that discussions are better if you keep them pleasant.

The second kind of relation, which is more commonly introduced at a later age, is called "concept-oriented." In this communicatory environment the child is stimulated to express his ideas; he is exposed to controversy and encouraged to join it. As with the socio-orientation measure, frequency and emphasis estimates by parent and child were summed across many items to provide a single index of concept-orientation. Sample items:

(1) (Parent) encourages (child) to challenge (parent's) ideas and beliefs.

(2) (Parent) asks (child's) opinion when family is discussing something.

(3) (Parent and child) have family talks about topics like politics or religion, where some persons take different sides from others.

(4) (Parent) says that (child) should always look at both sides of an issue before making up (child's) mind.

(5) (Parent) argues about things like politics or religion when visiting with friends or relatives, when (child) is present.

Table 2 shows that the socio-orientation decreases during adolescence. Concept-orientation changes very little from junior to senior high school. At both grade levels, about as many families stress *both* or *neither* orientation as stress one or the other.

Theoretically, it is the structure, not the specific content, of parent-child communication that the child learns to generalize. (We have found rather little evidence of the direct transmission of specific content, such as ideological values, from parent to adolescent–just as we find little evidence of direct media use modeling.) Further, the various combinations of these factors produce structural patterns that are not simply the sums of their two constituent parts. Therefore, we will discuss the family communication patterns in terms of a four-fold typology (see Table 2):

Laissez faire families emphasize neither type of relation. Children are not prohibited from challenging parental views but neither are they exposed to the world of independent and contending ideas.

Protective families stress sociorelations only. The child is encouraged to get along with others, at the expense of concept-relations that would expose him to the controversial world of ideas. Not only is he prohibited from expressing dissent, but he is given little chance to encounter information on which he might base his own views.

Pluralistic families emphasize the development of strong and varied concept-relations in an environment comparatively free of social restraints. The child is encouraged to explore new ideas and is exposed to controversial material; he can make up his own mind without fear of endangering social relations with his parents.

Consensual families attempt to stress both orientations. While the child is exposed to controversy, and told he should enter into it, he is paradoxically constrained to develop concepts that are consonant with existing sociorelations. That is, he is in effect encouraged to learn his parents' ideas and adopt their values.

For comparability between tables and measures, the media use measures have been converted to standard scores in Tables 3 (parents) and 4 (adolescents), setting the mean of the four raw scores within each row at zero (see notes to tables).

Looking first at the parent's media use, Table 3 shows several divergences. (For statistical inference, a standard score of about ±15 or greater can be considered significantly different from the overall score for the remaining groups at the .05 level in Tables 3 and 4.) The most distinctive difference is that between protective parents, who use television heavily and are low in news consumption, and pluralistic parents, who show the opposite pattern of media use. Consensual parents tend to be high on all media use indices, and laissez faire parents are consistently below average. These latter relationships could be due to response-set

TABLE 3
PARENT'S MEDIA USE (standard scores) BY FAMILY COMMUNICATION PATTERNS

Media Use Index		Family Communication Pattern: Laissez faire	Protec-tive	Plural-istic	Consen-sual	Mean Raw Score Overall
Parent's TV Time	Jr.Hi	00	+19	-23	+03	**1.72**
	Sr.Hi	-18	+27	-10	+11	**1.64**
Parent's TV Entertainment	Jr.Hi	-08	+22	-18	+04	**8.15**
	Sr.Hi	-12	+04	+05	+05	**9.06**
Parent's TV News	Jr.Hi	-06	-15	+12	+08	**10.05**
	Sr.Hi	-26	-05	+16	+16	**10.34**
Parent's News Reading	Jr.Hi	-11	-33	+25	+16	**15.35**
	Sr.Hi	-19	-23	+18	+22	**15.68**
(Number of cases)	Jr.Hi	(161)	(145)	(138)	(197)	(641)
	Sr.Hi	(184)	(131)	(179)	(156)	(650)

NOTE: Standard score entries are based on weighted means, setting the overall mean at zero and the standard deviation at unity, within each row. Scores are calculated to two decimal places; decimals are omitted for simplicity. The overall (bold) means at the right are index scores that are meaningful only for Junior High versus Senior High comparisons within each category. They are not comparable to the child's raw scores in Table 4, except for the TV Entertainment index.

toward questions about the frequency of occurrence of events in the home; but they could also indicate real correlations in the amount of at-home communication, via media versus with adolescents.

The righthand column of Table 3 shows the mean raw scores on each index for each parental cohort. There appear to be no major differences by grade level, except for the TV Entertainment measure. More detailed analysis showed that this difference is entirely due to heavier viewing of comedy programs by parents of the senior high students. There are some differences between grade levels in Table 3, within family communication types, but almost all are within the range of sampling error. In all, we can conclude that the parents of senior high students do not differ substantially from junior high parents, in media use patterns.

Turning to the adolescent's media use in Table 4 (righthand column), greater overall shifts in the mean raw scores can be seen. There is a clear developmental drop in general TV use and a strong increase in News Reading. The mild decrease in TV News consumption seems especially slight when considered in the context of the large general reduction in TV

TABLE 4
CHILD'S MEDIA USE (standard scores) BY FAMILY COMMUNICATION PATTERNS

Media Use Index		Family Communication Pattern: Laissez faire	Protective	Pluralistic	Consensual	Mean Raw Score Overall
Adolescent's TV Time	Jr.Hi	+02	+35	-38	-01	**5.22**
	Sr.Hi	+08	+22	-18	-07	**3.93**
Adolescent's TV Entertainment	Jr.Hi	+02	+08	-15	+03	**11.09**
	Sr.Hi	-07	+16	-04	00	**9.81**
Adolescent's TV News	Jr.Hi	-21	-15	+11	+21	**14.83**
	Sr.Hi	-22	-06	+14	+17	**14.47**
Adolescent's News Reading	Jr.Hi	-16	-35	+20	+25	**9.67**
	Sr.Hi	-19	-09	+15	+14	**11.47**
(Number of cases)	Jr.Hi	(161)	(145)	(138)	(197)	(641)
	Sr.Hi	(184)	(131)	(179)	(156)	(650)

NOTE: Standard score entries are based on weighted means, setting the overall mean at zero and the standard deviation at unity, within each row. Scores are calculated to two decimal places; decimals are omitted for simplicity. The overall (bold) means at the right are index scores that are meaningful only for Junior High versus Senior High comparisons within each category. They are not comparable to the parent's raw scores in Table 3, except for the TV Entertainment index.

Time. All these trends are roughly in keeping with earlier findings (e.g., Schramm et al., 1961). As was the case with parents, the differences between grade-level cohorts for adolescents within family communication types in Table 4 are almost all nonsignificant. Although there are some intriguing patterns, we would not hazard any important developmental inferences on the basis of these data.

The influence of family communication patterns on adolescent media use is rather clear in Table 4. The protective-pluralistic distinction is very much like that of the parents (Table 3). Adolescents in pluralistic homes give considerable attention to media news reports and spend relatively little time with television; the protective adolescent is a heavy television user but shows little interest in news (at least at the junior high level).

Neither the laissez faire nor the consensual adolescents differ much from the norm in general television use. But in media news consumption, they behave very much in accordance with the concept-orientation in the home. That is, the laissez faire group is about as low as the protectives in news use, and the consensuals are at least as high as the pluralistics. In the case of TV News, the laissez faire and consensual adolescents are the most extreme groups. The data for these two groups of youngsters in Table 4 cannot (unlike their parents) plausibly be ascribed to response-set, since their patterns for TV Time are somewhat in the direction opposite to a response-set prediction.

All in all, however, the standard scores for adolescents in Table 4 are strikingly similar to the corresponding data for their parents (Table 3). Comparing only the direction (plus versus minus) of the scores, this similarity of pattern is significant at the .01 level by sign test. Thus, although the modeling correlations based on comparisons within each family (Table 1) are weak and not very supportive of a direct-influence modeling interpretation, it appears that families with similar parent-child communication structures indirectly produce characteristic media use patterns that are shared by parent and adolescent—on the average. The parent-child communication milieu perhaps operates as a separate factor that independently leads parent and adolescent to behave similarly in other communication situations involving mass media.

This interaction between interpersonal and mass communication behavior is elaborated in Table 5, which shows the modeling correlations for each index by family communication type. These correlations are rather uniformly low for News Reading and high for TV Time, regardless

TABLE 5

PARENT-CHILD MEDIA USE CORRELATIONS WITHIN CATEGORIES BY FAMILY COMMUNICATION PATTERNS

Media Use Index		Family Communication Pattern			
		Laissez faire	Protective	Pluralistic	Consensual
TV Time	Jr.Hi	.09	.00	.11	.27
	Sr.Hi	.13	.30	.21	.17
TV Entertainment	Jr.Hi	.09	.41	.01	.21
	Sr.Hi	.00	.14	.01	.16
TV News	Jr.Hi	.07	.19	.09	.11
	Sr.Hi	.10	.28	-.08	.16
News Reading	Jr.Hi	.07	.02	-.03	.07
	Sr.Hi	-.03	.07	.06	.05
(Number of cases)	Jr.Hi	(161)	(145)	(138)	(197)
	Sr.Hi	(184)	(131)	(179)	(156)

NOTE: Cell entries are Pearson rs, and correspond to the bold entries on the main diagonal in Table 1.

of family communication pattern. These findings are consistent with our earlier inferences (above) that reading is not a behavior that is likely to be modeled and that simple exposure to a tuned-in television set can occur as a function of mere opportunity, without behavioral modeling.

For specific types of television content (entertainment and news), however, Table 5 indicates that any modeling that occurs is limited to those families in which there has been a strong socio-orientation—the protectives and consensuals. Although these two types of family differ in their patterns of television use (see Tables 3 and 4), the emphasis they share on social constraints on the developing child apparently serves as a cue for adolescent modeling of this overt behavior. In the protective home, the adolescent seems to follow the parental lead of heavy entertainment viewing and little news viewing; in the consensual home, the same basic social contingency coupled with the opposite parental viewing pattern is associated with the opposite adolescent viewing pattern.

The only hint of a developmental trend in Table 5 occurs for TV Entertainment and TV News among the socio-oriented families. In both the protective and consensual groups, the evidence of TV Entertainment modeling decreases from junior high to senior high, while the TV News modeling correlation increases modestly. These developmental shifts correspond to the overall changes in media use norms during adolescence—toward less entertainment and more news consumption—as the youngsters shift to more adult media behavior patterns. That is, early in adolescence, when the youngster spends much more time with television than his parents do, his exposure to entertainment programs is correlated with that of his parents—if the socio-orientation in the home is strong. Later in adolescence, as he begins to pay more attention to news reports, his use of television for this kind of information is associated more with parental example—again only when there is a strong socio-orientation between parent and child.

If one were to make value judgments regarding family communication patterns, the inclination would almost certainly be to prefer the pluralistic pattern. In other studies, we have found the adolescent from a pluralistic home to be more knowledgeable about public affairs, to make better grades in school (while spending less time with homework), to be more active in school and political activities, and (surprisingly) to want to be more like his parents than are youngsters from the other three types of homes (Chaffee et al., 1966; McLeod et al., 1967). In this study, we find that, despite the absence of direct modeling influences, the pluralistic adolescents end up using the mass media primarily for news and comparatively little for "escape" entertainment–much as their parents do. Similar findings, using somewhat different measures of family communication patterns, have been reported by Kline et al. (1970) in studies of two Minnesota samples. In an intensive study of black families in an urban ghetto, Nwankwo (1970) found pluralistic adolescents closer to their parents in relation to several issues, both in terms of perceived agreement and in terms of accurate perception of their parents' views. In a persuasion experiment, Eswara (1968) found that students from pluralistic homes were more sensitive to variations in the amount of information supporting an argument; that is, they appeared more "rational" and less easily persuaded than the other students. And pluralistics among college journalism students are more inclined to consider the content, as opposed to the source, of a persuasive message (Stone and Chaffee, 1970).

In this study, we find that adolescents in consensual homes report about as much attention to media news reports as do the pluralistic youths. But the results of this exposure are not equivalent in the two cases. In other analyses of data from this study, and in earlier studies (McLeod et al., 1967), we have found that the consensual adolescents score substantially lower than pluralistics on tests of knowledge of current news events and personalities. And in an earlier study (Chaffee et al., 1966) the consensual adolescents had earned the lowest grades in school social studies courses–despite spending more time (self-reported) with homework than any other group. In summary, the product of a consensual home appears to put more into public affairs information-seeking (via media and in school) but gets less out of it.

IMPLICATIONS FOR COMPARATIVE RESEARCH

It might be argued that a pluralistic family environment is the ideal one to prepare citizens for a pluralistic society. The same may not be true, however, for developing nations, where the system is not yet geared to a fully participant citizenry. Similarly, a pluralistic communication style might be poorly suited to underdeveloped sectors of American society. Combining some empirical evidence with anecodotal observations, we have concluded that pluralistic families are less likely to be found in low-income areas and in underdeveloped nations than in the kinds of working- and middle-class communities where most of our studies have been conducted (including the one reported in this paper).

When we have controlled statistically for socioeconomic status (McLeod et al., 1967), we have found that family communication patterns partially overlap status differences, but that each of these factors accounts for a separate portion of the total variance in media use and other indicators of adolescent development. Whether family communication structure "causes" differences in socioeconomic and political development or vice versa and whether mass media use is an integral factor or simply an external indicator of these processes remains to be investigated. That task will require comparative analyses of macrosocial systems that vary considerably in modal family type, socioeconomic and political attributes, and systems of mass communication.

REFERENCES

BOTTORFF, A. (1970) "Television, respect, and the older adolescent." Master's thesis. University of Wisconsin.

CHAFFEE, S. H., J. M. McLEOD, and C. K. ATKIN (1970) "Parent-child similarities in television use." Presented to Assn. for Education in Journalism, Washington, D.C.

CHAFFEE, S. H., J. M. McLEOD, and D. B. WACKMAN (1966) "Family communication and political socialization." Presented to Assn. for Education in Journalism, Iowa City, Iowa.

CHAFFEE, S. H., L. S. WARD, and L. P. TIPTON (1970) "Mass communication and political socialization in the 1968 campaign." Journalism Q. 47 (Winter).

CLARKE, P. (1969a) "Parental print use, social contact about reading and use of the print media by teenage boys." Presented to Pacific Chapter, American Assn. for Public Opinion Research, Napa, Calif.

--- (1969b) "Identification with father and father-son similarities in reading behavior." Presented to Assn. for Education in Journalism, Berkeley, Calif.

--- (1963) "An experiment to increase the audience for educational television." Ph.D. dissertation. University of Minnesota.

ESWARA, H. (1968) "An interpersonal approach to the study of social influence: family communication patterns and attitude change." Ph.D. dissertation. University of Wisconsin.

GREENBERG, B. S. and J. R. DOMINICK (1968) "Television usage, attitudes and functions for low-income and middle-class teenagers." Report 4, Project CUP (Communication Among the Urban Poor). East Lansing: Michigan State University.

HESS, R. D. and H. GOLDMAN (1962) "Parents' views of the effect of television on their children." Child Development 33: 411-426.

HIMMELWEIT, H. T., A. N. OPPENHEIM, and P. VINCE (1958) Television and the Child. London: Oxford Univ. Press.

KLINE, F. G., D. K. DAVIS, R. OSTMAN, L. VUORI, N. CHIRISTIANSEN, S. GUNARATNE, and L. KIVENS (1970) "Family and peer socialization and autonomy related to mass media use, mass institution evaluation and radical political activism: a descriptive analysis." Presented to International Assn. for Mass Communication Research, Constance, Germany.

McLEOD, J. M., S. H. CHAFFEE, and H. ESWARA (1966) "Family communication patterns and communication research." Presented to Assn. for Education in Journalism, Iowa City, Iowa.

McLEOD, J. M., S. H. CHAFFEE, and D. B. WACKMAN (1967) "Family communication: and updated report." Presented to Assn. for Education in Journalism, Boulder, Colo.

McLEOD, J. M., R. R. RUSH and K. H. FRIEDERICH (1968-1969) "The mass media and political information in Quito, Ecuador." Public Opinion Q. 32 (Winter); 575-587.

NWANKWO, R. (1970) "A perspective on family communication patterns and role-taking in an urban sub-culture." Ph.D. dissertation. University of Wisconsin.

SCHRAMM, W., J. LYLE, and E. B. PARKER (1961) Television in the Lives of Our Children. Stanford: Stanford Univ. Press.

STONE, V. A. and S. H. CHAFFEE (1970) "Family communication patterns and source-message orientation." Journalism Q. 47 (Summer): 239-246.

Adolescents, Creativity, and Media

An Exploratory Study

SERENA E. WADE
San Jose State College

Most previous survey research on children's or adolescents' media behavior has dealt almost exclusively with frequencies of media use, with program preferences, with various descriptive breakdowns of media behavior, and with displacement effects on one medium brought about by attention to another. Today, when media are abundantly available and the user must exercise some choice, a count of viewing hours or of items read does not answer some important questions about the kinds of programs or stories selected by individuals of different psychological characteristics, nor does it tell very much about how the individual integrates his choices into other activities.

The exploratory study reported here investigates the behavior of adolescents (with special focus on the creative adolescent) as active agents in the selection of media and integration of materials within media. The study had two goals: an exploration of media use by adolescents and tests of specific relationships between creativity and selected aspects of media behavior.

The focus on the adolescent emerges for several reasons. First, Himmelweit et al. (1958) and Schramm et al. (1961) have indicated that the media patterns which appear to be suggestive of adult behavior emerge at approximately grade ten; these patterns merit attention as symptomatic/diagnostic of maturing communication behavior.

In addition, a focus on adolescent behavior establishes a conservative test of observed relationships between psychological characteristics and use of leisure time. Academic and social demands are increasing during this period, placing constraints on the adolescent's available time. Any media use patterns must be conspicuous to be identifiable. Last, the creative adolescent as a special and atypical case has not been the subject of any previous media research.

CREATIVITY AND MEDIA BEHAVIOR

Creativity is a process of conscious manipulation of the environment that results in its redefinition in a unique manner. Creativity results when abundant ideas and observations (fluency) are freely exploited for their relational possibilities (flexibility) in the development of something unique (originality). Originality implies no value judgment regarding quality.

Three tests of divergent thinking were selected from the pioneer work of J. P. Guilford and his colleagues as the operational definition of creativity in this study.[1] These measures allowed subjects the freedom to exercise cognitive faculties within a semistructured, but malleable, framework–the type of environment that stimulates divergent thinking. This study considered creativity an exclusive cognitive property of the individual in interaction with the environment. Personality and culture were considered mediating variables, elements which either facilitate or thwart creativity but are not elements of creativity per se.

The relationship of creativity to media behavior lies in its influence as a psychological variable on the selection of media and materials within media; in this study, no attempt was made to determine the effects of media on creativity.[2] The emphasis on adolescent behavior as a function of the degree of creativity implies the manifestation of the essential elements of creativity–fluency, flexibility, and originality–in media behavior as well as elsewhere in adolescent activities. The importance in creativity lies in its possible prediction of behaviors different from those predicted by other psychological or environmental variables so commonly studied by media researchers.

By definition, the creative adolescent should be highly aware of his surroundings, able to consume and reproduce a large amount of material from media or other sources, and able to interrelate this material with great facility. He may be particularly interested in unusual or potentially redefinable things.

The implications of these characteristics for media behavior are interesting. It has been suggested that high and low media users may have some difficulty in aligning mental ability with aspirations (Schramm et al., 1961). While this may be applicable in the case of the creative youngster, it may well be a different kind of incompatibility—creativity may lead in directions that are not sanctioned by the achievement ethic.

Second, creativity may work against the "reality" pattern identified by Schramm and his colleagues. Stereotypes to the contrary, Torrance (1962) has found the social adjustments of the creative child to be quite stable, so that the need to escape into fantasy because of social inadequacies should not be present.

What remains when the reality and fantasy patterns are rendered less probable is an imaginative reconstruction of potential creative outlets. Himmelweit maintains that tastes in all media are usually similar. In contrast to this consistent behavior, the creative adolescent may so fill his time with independent efforts that media attention may be determined by entirely different criteria. Previous research tends to demonstrate a behavior pattern in creative persons that emphasizes variety, a need for something different or unpredictable (Houston and Mednick, 1963; Garlington and Shimota, 1964). A need for novelty might manifest itself in a pattern of variety when both print and visual media are considered as aggregate.[3]

In general, this study hypothesized that the creative adolescent would make only limited use of the media because he is committed to varied activities in his leisure hours, of which media are a small part (fluency). The creative adolescent was thought to be more diversified in his selections within media (originality), and he would tend to integrate media materials more fully into his daily life (flexibility). Selection of activities (including media) on the part of the creative youngster should show a large appetite which media fare might satisfy or increase. The predictability of media materials (particularly TV programs) might be annoying to the creative youngster.

Selection was defined as the number of independent media choices, those not related by content characteristics. Integration was defined as the number of uses to which media materials were put; the greater the frequency of applications, the greater the integration of the materials. Selection provides at least indirect evidence to support the hypothesized "need for novelty" in the creative youngster.

WEDDING THE TRADITIONS

The dovetailing of adolescent uses of media and the study of creativity appears to lead to the same types of variables. In both cases, behavior is affected by what the child brings within himself to the media and the particular conditions under which attention is given. Clearly identifiable variables include the antecedent creativity and the consequent media selection and integration, also intelligence and general activity preferences. These latter variables, among others, have served well as predictors of media behavior and as correlates of creativity, whether measured by test or overt behavior. This study has attempted to use these already identified variables as guides in the exploration of a new research area through survey.

The study sample of adolescents included 105 high school sophomores from two upper-middle-class communities in the San Francisco Bay Area. The students were tested for creative "potential" (divergent thinking) using the three Guilford tests whose interscorer reliabilities averaged .91. Each student completed a questionnaire containing items on leisure time activities in general, specific media behavior, media selection procedures, integration of media materials into other cognitive and behavioral patterns, and home environment. The research was primarily interested in establishing the relationship between creativity and adolescent media behavior; therefore, every effort was made to make maximum use of the data with correlational statistics. Exploration of hypotheses was informal and frankly tentative.

PREDICTION OF ADOLESCENT LEISURE ACTIVITIES

The creativity tests measured relatively independent factors; their cumulative total was correlated with verbal intelligence at .36 $p < .001$), indicating some cognitive overlap between the two measures and requiring subsequent partialling for the study of creativity and media behavior.[4] Both cognitive measures were equally efficient in predicting school achievement, but the predictions of leisure activity were quite different.

As can be seen from Table 1, correlations between the number of clubs and hobbies were significantly positive while those between creativity and TV were negative. When intelligence was removed, the relationship between creativity and print changed to zero. The correlation of intelligence and print use was .73 $p < .0001$). Clearly, the reality media use pattern is based on only one type of cognitive function (convergent thinking).

The inquiry into a need for novelty within the media showed a trend toward increased variety of content used with increased creativity. A score

TABLE 1
CORRELATIONS BETWEEN CREATIVITY AND LEISURE ACTIVITIES

Pearson r Coefficients for Total Creativity Score and	Zero-Order	p	Intelligence Removed	p
Clubs/hobbies	.439	$<.001$	.433	$<.001$
Print hours/week	.238	$<.01$	-.046	n.s.
TV hours/week	-.290	.001	-.290	.001
n = 103				

was created representing the number of different media materials children had attended "yesterday."[5] When this index was dichotomized at the median, and creativity scores were divided into three groups approximating a normal curve, the chi-square relationship between the two was significant at .10.

Media variety also increased with amount of time spent, yet higher creativity scores were consistently associated with less media time, indicating a higher variety-per-time unit than was the case for less creative youngsters. These data provide evidence that exposure to opportunities for easy flow of ideas and observations (fluency) in creative youngsters is observable in leisure activities. Creative youngsters expose themselves to more opportunities for different ideas and display greater desire for competing points of view in their selection variety among the mass media.

Questions on media choices were designed to take into account the differences between unplanned, referred, directed, and habitual media selection on the part of the creative adolescent as compared to his less creative peer.[6] The types of selection for each medium were scored on a continuum of random (4) to habitual (1) behavior; the range of scores was six to twenty for five questions, with an approximately normal score distribution.

The heavy occupation of the creative adolescent with clubs and hobbies has the effect of making his daily media selection procedure extremely random. High intelligence was negatively correlated with selection mode ($-.36/p < .001$), indicating a trend toward highly directed, planned behavior as intelligence increases. Partialling intelligence out of the creativity/selection correlation produced .46, significant at the .001 level.

The random mode of selection so strongly associated with creativity occurs regularly when the creative adolescent is confronted with daily media such as TV and newspapers. It is the selection of these daily media that differentiates highly creative youngsters from their peers. Selection of movies and books is made on some other basis, frequently friend or family recommendations, by all teenagers, regardless of creativity. Habitual attention to all media was more often reported by adolescents with low creativity and intelligence scores.

The need for novelty hypothesized in creative persons should be most readily observed when selection leads to an unsatisfactory experience. The subjects were asked whether they would remain with the selected medium and shift attention to other parts or would leave the field altogether should their initial selection prove disappointing. Table 2 shows a greater tendency to change activities totally with an increase in creativity. The varied selection patterns and clear need for novelty provide evidence on originality in creative youngsters.

Finally, applications of media materials to other activities attempted to cover only the most easily identifiable types of integration in the lives of adolescents–discussion and recommendation of media with family and friends. With intelligence partialled out, the data indicate that an increase in creativity is positively associated with an increase in discussions (.34/p < .01) but not related at all to the number of recommendations (.07 n.s.). The correlation of intelligence with discussion indicates a decline in media conversations with an increase in intelligence (-.29/p=.01), accompanied by an increase in recommendations with higher intelligence (.60 /p < .001). An increase in creativity seems to point toward gregarious behavior (discussion) while an increase in intelligence leans toward influential behavior (recommendation). Integration of media experiences into other activities provides evidence of flexibility in highly creative youngsters.

TABLE 2
PERCENTAGE REPORTING TENDENCY TO CHANGE BY CREATIVITY GROUP

	Creativity		
Reported Behavior	Low (n = 20)	Medium (n = 64)	High (n = 21)
Stay with medium	94	88	66
Change activities	6	12	34
$X^2 = 7.66$ p = .02 df = 2[a]			

a. Two expected cell frequencies fell below 5.

THE NATURE-NATURE QUESTION IN CREATIVITY

Rogers (1962) puts forth some conditions fostering creativity: psychological safety and psychological freedom. By safety, he means providing a climate in which external evaluation is not restrictive; by psychological freedom, he means the extent to which symbolic expression is fostered. If Rogers is right, then the home environment in which there are few restrictions on fantasy behavior (for instance, TV viewing) and perceived approval of varied experiences should be the environment in which creativity is fostered.

In their pioneer study, Getzels and Jackson (1961) concluded that parents of creative adolescents are more interested in less visible characteristics, such as openness to experience, values, and interests and enthusiasms. The highly creative family is one in which individual divergence is permitted and risks are accepted. By contrast, parents of high IQ children are more "vigilant" with respect to their children and school, more concerned with desirable qualities possessed by their children's friends. The association of increased parent SES level and disapproval of fantasy behavior has been found in several studies on media behavior (Maccoby, 1964).

Consequently, when this study selected subjects in an upper-middle-class area, disapproval of TV viewing as wasteful should have been expected; yet, when the association of home environment and creativity level was explored, some interesting findings supported Rogers' hypotheses regarding the type of environment that should serve as a mediating variable in the development of creativity.

Professional homes generally produced higher creativity scores. However, perceived approval of fantasy behavior was associated with higher

TABLE 3
MEAN CREATIVITY AND VERBAL INTELLIGENCE LEVELS SHOWING POSSIBLE ENVIRONMENT EFFECTS

		Father Professionally Employed (n = 34)	Father Nonprofessional (n = 62)
Perceived parent approval of time with TV (n = 52)	Creativity	108.12	85.05
	Intelligence	114.17	112.63
Perceived parent disapproval of time with TV (n = 44)	Creativity	84.21	73.34
	Intelligence	112.60	110.09

creativity scores in both professional and nonprofessional homes. When the same classifications were made for intelligence scores and perceived approval of TV viewing, little relationship was shown involving either parental attitude or father's occupation. These data indicate again that there is common ground between intelligence and creativity which ought not be ignored in further creativity research. But there is also reason to suspect that creativity is fostered by a particular type of environment which has little effect on intelligence. The correlation between intelligence and creativity can easily be attributed to common factors involved; the remaining variance appears to depend on the psychological safety and freedom in which the child is encouraged to present himself as an independent individual.

CONCLUSIONS

The leisure time of the creative adolescent is full. That time which is not occupied by the demands of the school is taken up with specific individual or group activities. The creative adolescent is a "joiner"; he is also a hobbyist—a collector, a musician, an artist, and frequently a sportsman. He pursues life with enthusiasm and shuns edited experience. He reads about as much, watches TV less, and generally exposes himself to more highly diversified activities (including media) than his less creative peers.

When the creative adolescent does seek out media for information or entertainment, he exhibits differential patterns. Daily media selection is done on a random basis while selection that implies more investment of time is done with reference to some reliable source, frequently friends or family. This is a good indicator of the value the creative adolescent accords time. When time and energy are left over from other pursuits, random selection of media requiring substantial time-energy investment would be inefficient. It is doubtful that these processes operate at the conscious level, but they are functional for the creative adolescent, and his selection patterns are clear. Perhaps this planning can be accounted for by the cognitive overlap between intelligence and creativity.

The creative adolescent is more gregarious than most; he shares much of his leisure time with others, as indicated by his membership in a large number of clubs and other organizations. He also shares his media experiences with others, both friends and family, through frequent discussion of media. This tendency toward openness undoubtedly is encouraged by the home environment of the creative adolescent. From the small clues revealed in this study, the parents of creative adolescents are well educated, interested in, and supportive of their children.

QUESTIONS THAT STILL NEED ANSWERS

While this study has concentrated on selected aspects of creativity's influence on media behavior, other factors also may be important. Some additional attention might well be paid to family media patterns: The question of actual media control in large families—not uncommon in the highly creative group—is a poignant one. Is the random selection a true correlate of creativity or is random selection an artifact of having to attend what has already been selected by others in the family after other, perhaps more interesting, activities have been exhausted? The relative influence of adults and children in selection is of interest not only where creative adolescents are concerned but as a key to media status in the general family routine.

It would also be of great interest to replicate with a large cross-sectional sample the investigation of the dependent media variables used in this study. A satisfactory explanation of the reversals in predictions made by creativity and intelligence deserves some additional attention.

In the final analysis, however, the largest unknowns are the factors intrinsic to media presentations that appeal to the creative adolescent. It has been shown that he exposes himself to more different types of materials, but an extensive analysis of these materials needs to be done. In general, the creative adolescent sees and reads the same types of materials as do his peers, *plus* the additional special interest items which make his behavior different. He does not regularly select "quality" reading or TV programming (e.g., he does not watch much noncommercial TV). It would be valuable, both theoretically and practically, to know what variables make media interesting to adolescents in general, and creative adolescents in particular as an especially discerning audience. Knowing that some kinds of media materials do attract the attention of even the most active and inventive individuals, it would be of great interest to identify their underlying and common properties.

NOTES

1. These tests were Ideational Fluency, Alternate Use, and Consequences. See Christensen et al. (1958, 1960) and Christensen and Guilford (1957).

2. Research on media stimulation of creativity has not proved very fruitful in its results. Although Himmelweit et al. (1958) made no direct study of creativity, relevant findings include the following: TV provided only a slight gain in children's general knowledge–a net profit only for the younger, duller children; viewing stimulated interest rather than activity–the rapid succession of programs only stimulated children with initially strong interest in a given topic; viewers developed few new hobbies or interests as a result of TV. Schramm et al. (1961) found only incidental later use of TV experiences; the kinds of activities that resulted from TV were either fads or adapted details which fit into already existing interests.

3. As an alternative explanation for the relationship between creativity and need for novelty hypothesized here, some form of anxiety may result in general instability in the creative youngster. Divergent thinking has been unrelated to anxiety in two recent studies (Flescher, 1963; Feldhusen et al., 1965). Alexander (1964) maintains that because creativity may well be a higher form of play, it is probably free of the need to resolve tension immediately. The creative adolescent readily admits complexity and restructures apparently diverse stimuli.

4. Scores on the Lorge-Thorndike Verbal Ability Intelligence Test were provided by the schools.

5. Novelty in use of the media was measured by asking children to identify the name and type of content attended "yesterday." Mentions were coded for the variety of content, irrespective of the media in which it appeared. Thus, a respondent who watched TV news, then a western, followed by a symphony was rated higher in novelty than one who read a western novel, viewed a western TV show, and heard country-western music on the radio.

6. A sample question was:

What was the last TV program you saw yesterday? ______________________

How did you choose it? (CHECK ONLY ONE)

_4_ watched what someone else had already chosen

_3_ followed friend or family recommendations

_2_ used TV program guide to see what was on

_1_ always watch the same TV programs every week

REFERENCES

ALEXANDER, F. (1964) "Neurosis and creativity." Amer. J. of Psychoanalysis 24: 116-130.

ANDERSON, H. H. [ed.] (1959) Creativity and Its Cultivation: Addresses Presented at the Interdisciplinary Symposia on Creativity. New York: Harper & Row.

CHRISTENSEN, P. R. and J. P. GUILFORD (1957) Ideational Fluency I, Form A. Beverly Hills: Sheridan Supply.

CHRISTENSEN, P. R., P. R. MERRIFIELD, and J. P. GUILFORD (1958) Consequences. Beverly Hills: Sheridan Supply.

--- and R. C. WILSON (1960) Alternate Uses, Form A. Beverly Hills: Sheridan Supply.

FELDHUSEN, J. F., T. DENNY, and C. F. CONDON (1965) "Anxiety, divergent thinking, and achievement." J. of Educational Psychology 56 (February): 40-45.

FLESCHER, I. (1963) "Anxiety and achievement of intellectually gifted and creatively gifted children." J. of Psychology 56 (October): 251-268.

GARLINGTON, W. K. and H. E. SHIMOTA (1964) "The change-seeker index: a measure of the need for variable stimulus input." Psych. Reports 14 (June): 919-924.

GETZELS, J. W. and P. W. JACKSON (1961) "Family environment and cognitive styles: a study of the sources of highly intelligent and of highly creative adolescents." Amer. Soc. Rev. 26 (June): 351-359.

HIMMELWEIT, H. T., A. N. OPPENHEIM, and P. VINCE (1958) Television and the Child. London: Oxford Univ. Press.

HOUSTON, J. P. and S. A. MEDNICK (1963) "Creativity and the need for novelty." J. of Abnormal and Social Psychology 66 (February): 137-141.

MACCOBY, E. E. (1964) "Effects of mass media." Review of Child Development Research I. New York: Russell Sage.

ROGERS, C. R. (1962) "Toward a theory of creativity," in S. J. Parnes and H. F. Harding (eds.) A Source Book for Creative Thinking. New York: Charles Scribner.

SCHRAMM, W., J. LYLE, and E. B. PARKER (1961) Television in the Lives of Our Children. Stanford: Stanford Univ. Press.

TORRANCE, E. P. (1962) Guiding Creative Talent. Englewood Cliffs: Prentice-Hall.

Children's Response to Entertainment

Effects of Co-Orientation on Information-Seeking

PETER CLARKE
University of Michigan

The increased research attention being devoted to youth and entertainment culture results, in part, from the numerical and economic prominence of the teen market and from a growing appreciation of expressive values found in man's leisure.[1] By now, it is commonplace to observe that the values adolescents find in entertainment or the mass media are a function of group behavior–standing in the peer group, frequency of dating, parental values, and the like (Riley and Riley, 1951; Coleman, 1961; Clarke, 1965a; Chaffee et al., 1971). Yet, despite general discussions of group variables in the communication process (Riley and Flowerman, 1951; Freidson, 1953b; Klapper, 1960; Larsen, 1964), there have been surprisingly few efforts to advance a social-theoretical framework for studying children's entertainment choices or their responses to entertainment experiences.

Entertainment is a broad category and as difficult to define as leisure (for attempts, see de Grazia, 1962; Kaplan, 1960; Dumazedier, 1967). Included are popular media–such as the Top 40, movies, and television–and the performing arts–like symphony and theatre–that attract narrower

---

Author's Note: *The research reported here was supported by a grant from the U.S. Office of Education, and was conducted while the author was on the faculty of the University of Washington.*

audiences. Experiencing these entertainments is not simply an individual act; viewing and listening are more usually social behaviors undertaken in group settings (Freidson, 1953a; Johnstone, 1961; Clarke, 1965b, 1970b).

It follows that *responses to* entertainment, as well as *choice of* entertainment, may be a function of social expectations and perceptions. The purpose of this paper is to examine evidence of social, as opposed to individual, correlates of a distinct kind of response to entertainment—information-seeking.

This choice of dependent variable needs some explanation. Most research on entertainment behavior—record listening, television viewing, and so forth—has considered these experiences as communication and has looked for noncommunication consequences. These consequences include how much the entertainment was enjoyed (Steiner, 1963; Belson, 1967), the meanings ascribed to it (Wallach, 1964; Robinson and Hirsch, 1969), time displaced by it (Robinson, 1969), and behavior resulting from it (Katz and Foulkes, 1962).

We have been more interested in *communication consequences* of entertainment—specifically, whether or not a person seeks information about entertainment or its practitioners after exposure to a performance of the entertainment. Of course, information-seeking about entertainment can itself be entertaining. Reading movie gossip columns or record jackets, or tuning in disc jockeys are emotional as well as learning experiences. It is difficult to tell how the entertainment-information industry functions to reduce uncertainty about the subjects it covers, and how it functions to amuse or excite information seekers.

In any event, we wish to learn more about adolescents' information-seeking because this communication helps distinguish the active from the passive entertainment audience. At a minimum, seeking information increases the salience of an entertainment form or entertainers, and draws the topics more firmly within the life space of the individual.

The setting for the present discussion and research into information-seeking is not commercial entertainment but a performing art—the symphony concert. The Seattle Symphony travels to schools throughout Washington State as part of an arts educational program covering several performing media (including theatre, opera, and dance). Fifty-minute concerts are usually given in gyms before large audiences of youngsters bused to a centrally located school. To some children, the experience is new and forced. Others are excited by the event.

Research into children's reactions to the concerts has provided an opportunity to do four things: (1) to define a communicative response to the concert, information-seeking, that has wide relevance to other entertainment experiences, forced or voluntary, (2) to set forth a model for studying information-seeking that recognizes the social relevance of both entertainment and information about it, (3) to test some propositions using the model, and (4) to suggest implications of the model for the study of youth and entertainment culture generally.

CONCEPTS AND HYPOTHESES FOR STUDYING CHILDREN'S INFORMATION-SEEKING ABOUT ENTERTAINMENT

INFORMATION-SEEKING

A familiar way of analyzing information search is to take note of the use people make of mass media channels—in the case of entertainment, fan magazines, newspaper reviews, and similar outlets. Unfortunately, this approach confounds persons' search behavior with the availability of information in the environment. This problem is acute in the case of performing arts, where we might discover a considerable thirst for information that is being provided nowhere.

Accordingly, at least two definitions of information-seeking are worth distinguishing:

(1) Seeking is an expressed need to find out something, regardless of how available that "something" is.

(2) Seeking is taking advantage of a defined information opportunity, where access to the information is equal across persons.

We have conducted preliminary studies of the questions children ask about symphony and symphony musicians after attending concerts, and we have learned that the visibility of sources that might meet these information wants is very low. However, analysis of children's questions has helped in constructing information opportunities about symphony that can be made available to youngsters.

In the present study, separate measures of children's information-seeking are used for the two definitions above. Although we are dealing with symphony as an entertainment, the definitions are relevant to communicative response to any entertainment experience.

Co-orientation

Explanations for information-seeking are customarily sought on the level of personal characteristics, like education or sex. By contrast, we subscribe to a co-orientation model in which explanation is achieved on the level of a person's perceptions of his acquaintances and how they view the object of information.

Assumptions about the social nature of entertainment suggest the appropriateness of using a co-orientation model. Since there are few objective means by which individuals can judge the quality of entertainment, many persons engage in social comparisons about the event—they match their evaluations with others'. Social comparison increases the stability of one's evaluations (Festinger, 1950, 1954) and offers an occasion for expressing affection and other interpersonal rewards.

Thus, being entertained frequently results in social comparison activities like, "Did you enjoy the Bach?" or "Wasn't that a cool movie?" Co-orientation is often a consequence: One gets an idea of how others feel. The more co-orientation that is favorable about the entertainment, the more benefits a person can gain from information-seeking—if we assume that information facilitates further social comparison.

Co-orientation, as it is used here, means knowledge of how others evaluate an entertainment. Figure 1 shows variables in the model, which is patterned after Newcomb (1953).

Four concepts are specified by the model:

(1) Object of orientation. This is a discriminable entertainment within A's experience.[2]

(2) Person A's evaluation of the entertainment.

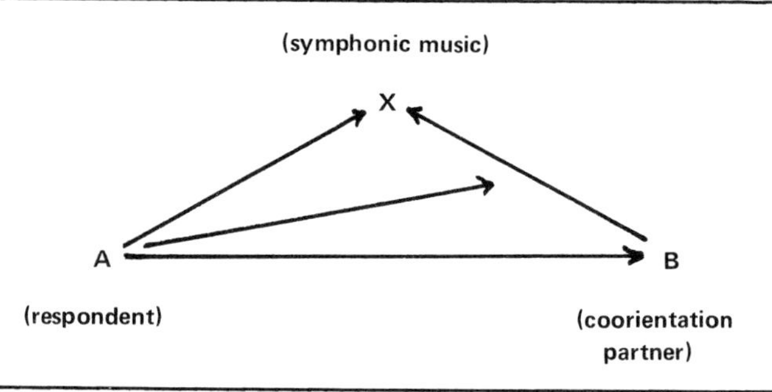

Figure 1. CO-ORIENTATION MODEL SHOWING VARIABLES USED IN THE PRESENT ANALYSIS.

(3) Co-orientation partner, B. This is any person whose entertainment evaluation is known by A.

(4) Perceived partner's evaluation, B-X.

One subsidiary concept can be added. This is whether or not an entertainment has been discussed between A and B.

The co-orientation model provides a means for systematically learning whether a person's social environment has evaluative connections with an entertainment and how the person perceives those connections, *if they exist.* A sociological concept like "reference group" can be accommodated by noting characteristics of co-orientation partners, such as whether they are parents or peers.[3] We analyze these two spheres separately below.

HYPOTHESES

The model's applicability to explaining information-seeking is illustrated by testing seven hypotheses:

Hypothesis 1. Information-seeking about an entertainment or its practitioners is positively correlated with favorable co-orientation toward the entertainment.

Hypothesis 2. Discussion with favorable co-orientation partners about the entertainment is positively correlated with information-seeking. To the extent that social comparison depends on social interaction that has already occurred, correlations tested in hypothesis 2 should be greater than those tested in hypothesis 1.

Hypothesis 3. Discussion about the entertainment, irrespective of the co-orientation status of discussants, correlates less with information-seeking than the independent variables contained in hypotheses 1 and 2.

Talking with others about a topic is not equivalent to learning their evaluations of it (see Watzlawick et al., 1967).

Hypothesis 4. Hypotheses 1-3 are tested separately for parent and peer spheres of relationship. The co-orientation model does not contain concepts describing role relationships, so predictions are not made as to which sphere correlates most with information-seeking. The supposed adult character of symphony might lead one to expect higher parent correlations for this entertainment. Studies posited on peer *versus* parent reference attachments (Rosen, 1955, 1955-1956; Bowerman and Kinch, 1959) might suggest higher peer correlations among teenage respondents.

Hypothesis 5. We wish also to test whether favorable co-orientation in each sphere–parents and peers–has an additive effect on information–seeking. If the effect is additive, children who have favorable co-orientations with both parents and peers should show greater levels of information-seeking than children who have favorable partners in only one sphere.

Hypothesis 6. Favorable co-orientation is empirically as well as theoretically distinct from a person's own evaluations of entertainment. Favorable co-orientation correlates positively with information-seeking, even when personal evaluations (A-X) of the entertainment are held constant.

Hypothesis 7. Co-orientation is not a symmetrical concept. The presence of partners who feel lukewarm (at best) about an entertainment does not in itself discourage information-seeking; the absence of a favorable partner does.

These hypotheses are straightforward. They state that youngsters' information-seeking about entertainment depends on whether acquaintances are thought to enjoy that entertainment. We are not sure whether the type of acquaintance matters, but for a start parents and peers will be distinguished.

Most important, taking account of children's perceptions of others' entertainment attitudes contributes an explanation of information-seeking not provided by children's own entertainment attitudes. Some children who are unenthused by symphony seek information because friends like the music.

Finally, acquaintances' disliking of an entertainment is not the opposite coin from liking in its effect on information-seeking.

METHODS

SAMPLE AND PROCEDURES

Data were collected four to five days after children had attended a Seattle Symphony concert at which works by Beethoven, Franck, Richard

Strauss, Antheil, and others were performed. Three hundred and twelve seventh,- ninth,- and eleventh-grade students from two suburban school districts near Seattle were included in the analysis.[4]

With one exception, the sample was drawn by selecting every nth name from school enrollment rosters. At one high school, eleventh graders were selected by drawing intact classes taking a required subject. The original sample contained 393 children. The reduction to 312 eliminates those who did not attend the school concert.

Questionnaires were administered to small groups of students by staff from the Communication Research Center. Anonymity was assured, and respondents did not write their names on questionnaires.

MEASURES OF INFORMATION-SEEKING

Information-seeking as a felt need to find out something, information wants, was measured by asking each child if there was "anything about symphony music or musicians that you would like to find out?" Mentions of performance or musical topics were coded. To qualify, a mention had to contain a noun-attribute linkage.

The second measure of seeking, taking advantage of an information opportunity, was obtained by including a booklet offer at the end of the questionnaire. Two booklets were offered: "Listening to Symphonies–a guide to understanding and enjoying symphonic music"; and "Seattle Symphony Musicians–how they got their training and how they work." Respondents were invited by the questionnaire to detach a stamped and addressed postcard, indicate which booklet they wanted, write their address, and mail the postcard.[5]

The two measures correlate (Gamma coefficient) at .50 ($z = 2.85$; $p < .01$).[6] Twenty-seven percent mentioned at least one information want, and 21% mailed for a booklet.

MEASURES OF CO-ORIENTATION AND CONCERT DISCUSSIONS

Items measuring the presence of co-orientation partners and perceived B-X evaluations appeared early in each child's questionnaire. The survey administrator read the following aloud, while children read it silently in the questionnaire:

> Without really knowing what other people think about things, we sometimes have an idea of what their feelings are about things. We would like you to think about music for a moment.
>
> Are there any persons whose likes and dislikes in music you feel you know something about?

Youngsters who marked "yes" listed persons by name and indicated who they were. Then they were asked to indicate which persons had attended the concert and to mark how much of the music they thought each person "liked–if he attended–or would have liked if he had attended." A scale was provided so that respondents could circle "almost all" the music, "most," "some," "very little," or "don't know."

Later in the questionnaire, children were asked if they had talked about the concert with anyone since they had attended it and to list these persons by name. Mentions of co-orientation partners and discussants were coded into five categories–parent, peers, siblings, teachers, and other adults.[7] The first two categories are used in the present analysis. Within each group–parents and peers–three indices were derived:

(1) The number of persons (parents or peers) the child thinks liked "almost all" of the music performed at the concert–favorable B-X perceived.

(2) The number of persons thought to like "almost all" of the music, with whom the child discussed the concert–favorable B-X talked with.

(3) The number of persons with whom the child discussed the concert, irrespective of whether they are co-orientation partners or not.

Distributions for these variables are shown in Table 1.

TABLE 1
DISTRIBUTION OF CO-ORIENTATION AND DISCUSSION VARIABLES

	Percentage of Children with at least One Parent Mention	Percentage of Children with at least One Peer Mention
Favorable B-X perceived	19	20
Favorable B-X talked with	11	12
Person talked with	42	64

MEASURE OF OWN CONCERT EVALUATION

To assess the A-X variable in the model, children were asked how much of the music they had liked—"almost all" to "very little."

RESULTS

HYPOTHESES 1-4

Table 2 contains Gamma correlations between co-orientation and information-seeking and discussion and information-seeking—separately by parents and peers. The appropriate z-values for reference to the normal curve are shown under each coefficient.

Since directional hypotheses are advanced, one-tail tests at the .05 level are applied to these data. (A z-value of 1.65 or greater indicates a statistically significant coefficient.)

TABLE 2
CORRELATIONS BETWEEN CO-ORIENTATION, DISCUSSION, AND INFORMATION-SEEKING, BY SOCIAL SPHERE

	Information-Seeking	
	Booklet	Want
Parent Variables		
Favorable B-X perceived	.44	.37
	(2.24)[a]	(1.91)[a]
Favorable B-X talked with	.37	.41
	(1.43)	(1.71)[a]
Person talked with	.17	.36
	(1.12)	(2.33)[b]
Peer Variables		
Favorable B-X perceived	.44	.51
	(2.27)[a]	(2.96)[b]
Favorable B-X talked with	.43	.48
	(2.62)[b]	(2.21)[a]
Person talked with	.15	.21
	(0.86)	(1.31)
n averages 300 cases		

a. $p < .05$.
b. $p < .01$.

Table 2 has been organized to show the set of parent variables, followed by corresponding peer variables. It can be seen that the presence of a favorable co-orientation partner correlates substantially with children's information-seeking. "Favorable B-X perceived" is significantly related to sending for a booklet and to information wants, whether the perception involves parents or peers.

Whether or not the child discussed the concert with his favorable co-orientation partners seems to make little differnece. Relationships involving "favorable B-X talked with" are about equal to those involving "favorable B-X perceived."

Finally, only one of the correlations between information-seeking and discussion about the concert is significant—the one between talking with parents and information wants.

HYPOTHESIS 5

Possible additivity of co-orientation on information-seeking requires additional analysis for testing. From the data already presented, it is clear that the strongest impact from co-orientation on information-seeking is perceiving others with favorable evaluations of symphony. Consequently, the test of hypothesis 5 is confined to this variable, "favorable B-X perceived."[8]

Table 3 contains percentages of children who sent for a booklet and who specified an information want within each of four groups—no

TABLE 3

PERCENTAGES OF INFORMATION SEEKERS, BY FAVORABLE B-Xs PERCEIVED

	Perception of at least One Favorable B-X			
	Neither Parent nor Peer	Parent Only	Peer Only	Both Parent and Peer
Percentage of booklet senders[a]	16	28	27	52
n =	(210)	(39)	(41)	(21)
Percentage with information want[b]	19	35	46	52
n =	(201)	(37)	(39)	(21)

a. Chi-square for booklet-sending equals 14.8; 3 d.f.; $p < .001$.

b. Chi-square for information wants equals 19.0; 3 d.f.; $p < .001$.

favorable B-X, parent-only favorable, peer-only favorable, and both parent and peer favorable.

For each dependent variable, the rates of information-seeking climb from fewer than one out of five among children with neither parent nor peer partners to around one out of two among children with both parent and peer partners who are favorable. Chi-squares are significant beyond the .001 level.

Table 3 shows mixed results concerning the additive nature of co-orientation. In the case of booklet-sending, children with both parent and peer partners are significantly more likely to have sent the postcard than children with only one partner (chi-square equals 4.5; 1 d.f.; $p < .05$). However, the difference in information wants between corresponding groups fails to attain statistical significance.

Hypothesis 6

A first step in comparing the explanatory power of attitudes toward entertainment and co-orientation is to examine correlations between each and information-seeking.

Two conveniences are employed in comparing the predictors. By now, it is clear that sending for a booklet and expressing an information want are two manifestations of the same variable. They correlate with each other, and they enter into parallel relationships with other variables (with the exception of hypothesis 5).

Consequently, a summary score was constructed for information behavior that reflects whether the respondent sent for a booklet and whether he expressed at least one information want. The score ranges from 0 to 2.

The second convenience is to sum the two co-orientation variables, favorable parent and favorable peer B-X, into a single index—again, ranging from 0 to 2.

The correlation between this favorable co-orientation score and information-seeking is .54 ($z = 3.79$; $p < .01$). This compares with a correlation of .42 ($z = 2.72$; $p < .01$) for the relationship between child's concert attitude and information-seeking.

The case for the co-orientation variable must rest on a second test, however. Children's attitudes toward the music are held constant while examining the correlation between co-orientation and information-seeking. Table 4 reports the results.

TABLE 4
CORRELATIONS BETWEEN CO-ORIENTATION AND INFORMATION-SEEKING, HOLDING CHILD'S CONCERT ATTITUDE CONSTANT

	Children who Liked "Almost All" or "Most" of the Music		
	Co-orientation:		
Information-seeking:	None	Some	
none	62%	38%	G = .45
some	38	62	(2.41)[a]
	100%	100%	
n =	(110)	(71)	
	Children who Liked Only "Some" or "Very Little" of the Music		
	Co-orientation:		
Information-seeking:	None	Some	
none	80%	50%	G = .60
some	20	50	(2.38)[a]
	100%	100%	
n =	(90)	(26)	

a. $p < .01$.

It can be seen that the relationship between co-orientation and information-seeking continues to be significant when concert attitude is held constant. The two coefficients have almost identical z-values, which are significant beyond the .01 level by one-tailed test. Even among children with comparatively negative attitudes toward the concert, the presence of a favorable co-orientation partner is strongly related to information-seeking.

Hypothesis 7

The presence of favorable co-orientation strongly correlates with information seeking. Is the presence of parents or peers who are thought to feel lukewarm (at best) about the music negatively related to booklet sending or information wants?

Within each sphere, parents and peers, each child was coded for the number of persons thought to like "very little" or "some" of the music performed at concert. A second index was also scored that reflects whether the child discussed the concert with any of these "unfavorable" partners.

For each index, in each sphere, the correlation with information-seeking is almost exactly zero. Our tentative conclusion is, therefore, that co-orientation is not symmetrical: The presence of favorable partners operates differently on information-seeking than the presence of unfavorable partners.

DISCUSSION AND IMPLICATIONS

Data reported here have a number of limitations. Only one entertainment form has been studied, and that is one for which large teenage audiences are mostly engineered, not voluntary. The effects of this arrangement on *relationships* between co-orientation and information-seeking are difficult to speculate. It is worth noting, however, that approximately four out of ten youngsters wanted information about symphony, even though the concert they attended was a public school event.

Another difference between symphony and more popular entertainments is the level of children's knowledge about performance and performers. We have not yet studied the *persistence* of information-seeking and its dependence on social perceptions.

Nor can we say anything about how repeated exposure to an entertainment form affects information-seeking. Concerts and other stagings of the performing arts are rare; few broadcast stations air reproductions. The uncertainty most children must face in looking ahead to future concerts may reduce their appetite for information and may alter the importance of co-orientation.

With these limitations in mind, the utility of a co-orientation model for explaining information-seeking about entertainment receives strong support on two counts—its absolute predictive power and the distinctiveness of variance explained. A variety of individual variables appropriate to the entertainment in this study were also measured—such as playing of musical instruments, participation in band or orchestra at school, viewing concerts on television, and the like. None of these accounts for as much variability in information-seeking as presence of favorable co-orientation partners.

One failure in the results concerns the presumed role of social comparison as a mediator variable. "Favorable B-X talked with" correlates about the same with information-seeking as "favorable B-X perceived." Perhaps one school concert is too limited a base of experience with symphony-as-entertainment to use in estimating the amount of social comparison with acquaintances. Or, much of the social comparison relevant to information-seeking may be anticipated, rather than past.

Despite this deficiency, co-orientation seems more potent, theoretically and empirically, as an explanation for information-seeking than a concept like social interaction. In Table 2, seven out of eight co-orientation relationships are significant, compared to one out of four involving discussion.

Data reported here have other implications for the study of children's leisure:

First, findings in Table 4, if replicated using other entertainments, emphasize a latent function served by information sources about performers and their art form. Celebrity magazines and other mass media not only satisfy the needs of entertainment fans; they are rewarding to nonfans as well—at least those nonfans who are aware of favorable co-orientation partners.

One image of the nonfan information seeker is that of a person adjusting to the enthusiasms of others. Perhaps he wants to ready himself for conversations with others, to make a good impression, to seek approval, or just find out more about things that acquaintances value.[9]

Much remains to be learned about characteristics of self-other relationships that mediate the importance of socially relevant information-seeking. The A-B link is an untapped dimension of the co-orientation model.

One appropriate variable is the generality of co-orientation with a partner—the range of entertainments or other topics about which B-Xs are known by A. One would suppose that the effects of co-orientation on information-seeking about a particular topic are more pronounced where A and B co-orient about many things, than where their relationship is specialized.

Other variables (from which co-orientation is derivative) include frequency of social contact with partners and the importance one places on the sentiments and values of partners.

Second, reference group theory, which usually distinguishes between adolescents' peer and parent attachments, may have relatively little to contribute to a study of children's information-seeking about entertainment. *Whom* the child co-orients with appears less important than the presence of a favorable partner—at least in the case of an elite entertainment, like symphony.

What seems to be recommended is theoretical reduction in which we abandon a sociological concept, role relationship, for a cognitive concept, co-orientation.

Third, the design of the study reported here establishes favorable co-orientation as antecedent to information-seeking. This suggests that information behavior might be sensitive to manipulations in social comparison and co-orientation experiences. If we wanted to increase children's information search about a particular entertainment, we might engineer social situations in which children could become aware of how others evaluated the entertainment.

Data showing that co-orientation is not symmetrical—that the absence of favorable partners is not equivalent to the presence of unfavorable partners—suggest that manipulated co-orientation is more likely to yield positive than negative results in information-seeking. We have field experiments underway dealing with these questions.

CONCLUSION

Communicative responses to entertainment have usually been neglected in studies of leisure among children and adults. This is surprising, since a great deal of mass media content portrays the world of entertainment, either fictionalized or "real." Social rewards obtained from using these media deserve to be studied in conjunction with research on entertainment behavior itself.

NOTES

1. Not all of this attention fits the traditional mold of survey-method social science. For examples of observational studies of youth culture, see Roszak (1969) and Wolfe (1968).

2. Any entertainment, especially symphonic music, is an ambiguous object of co-orientation to accommodate in a questionnaire. For many respondents, verbal labels and nonlinguistic sense categories do not match. In this circumstance, the safest approach in questioning persons is to point to a performance within their range of experience—in our case, the school concert.

3. To account for reference group completely, one needs to learn whether persons use their B-X perceptions in forming evaluations of entertainment. This question is not examined in the present report.

4. Ns reported in tables are somewhat smaller due to missing data on one or more variables.

5. The proportion of children who responded to this offer equals results in an earlier study in eastern Washington (Clarke, 1970a), where the offer was couched in different language and different materials were made available. Twenty-eight percent of the booklet senders wanted *Listening to Symphonies,* and 72% wanted *Seattle Symphony Musicians.* No distinction is made between these groups in the following analysis.

6. All correlations reported here are Gamma coefficients. For properties of this statistic, see Costner (1965).

7. Teachers and other adults were seldom cited as co-orientation partners. Siblings have been excluded from the present analysis, since the number of brothers and sisters in each child's family varies widely.

8. Parent- and peer-favorable co-orientation are correlated ($G = .47$; $z = 2.34$, $p < .01$). Children may live in a homogeneous social environment concerning symphony, or they may impose a degree of symmetry in how they perceive parents and friends.

9. There is another way to illustrate the importance of how acquaintances are thought to feel about entertainment, compared to one's personal evaluation. As mentioned earlier, data were gathered concerning children's postconcert conversations about the performance. Whether or not a youngster talked with a co-orientation partner about the concert is much more a function of favorability of the partner's attitude, than a function of the youngster's own attitude.

REFERENCES

BELSON, W. A. (1967) The Impact of Television. Hamden: Archon.

BOWERMAN, C. E. and J. W. KINCH, (1959) "Changes in family and peer orientation of children between the fourth and tenth grades." Social Forces 37 (March): 206-211.

CHAFFEE, S. H., J. M. McLEOD, and C. K. ATKIN (1971) "Parental influences on adolescent media use." Amer. Behavioral Scientist (January).

CLARKE, P. (1970a) "Children's information seeking about the symphony." Council for Research in Music Education, Bull. 19 (Winter): 1-15.

--- (1970b) "The social context of mass communication behavior." Presented at a conference on Youth and Change in Industrial Society: The Problem of Generations, October 15-18, Madison, Wisconsin.

--- (1965a) "Parental socialization values and children's newspaper reading." Journalism Q. 42 (Autumn): 539-546.

--- (1965b) "Increasing the audience for educational television." Audio-Visual Communication Rev. 13 (Summer): 183-195.

COLEMAN, J. S. (1961) The Adolescent Society. New York: Free Press.

COSTNER, H. L. (1965) "Criteria for measures of association." Amer. Soc. Rev. 30 (June): 341-353.

de GRAZIA, S. (1962) Of Time, Work, and Leisure. New York: Doubleday.

DUMAZEDIER, J. (1967) Toward a Society of Leisure. New York: Free Press.

FESTINGER, L. (1954) "A theory of social comparison processes." Human Relations 7: 117-140.
--- (1950) "Informal social communication." Psych. Rev. 57 (September): 271-282.
FREIDSON, E. (1953a) "The relation of the social situation of contact to the media in mass communication." Public Opinion Q. 17 (Summer): 230-238.
--- (1953b) "Communications research and the concept of the mass." Amer. Soc. Rev. 18 (June): 313-317.
JOHNSTONE, J. W. C. (1961) "Social sturcture and patterns of mass media consumption." Ph.D. dissertation. University of Chicago.
KAPLAN, M. (1960) Leisure in America: A Social Inquiry. New York: John Wiley.
KATZ, E. and D. FOULKES (n.d.) "On the use of mass media as 'escape': clarification of a concept." Public Opinion Q. 26 (Fall): 377-388.
KLAPPER, J. T. (1960) The Effects of Mass Communication. Glencoe: Free Press.
LARSEN, O. N. (1964) "Social effects of mass communication," pp. 348-381 in R. E. L. Faris (ed.) Handbook of Modern Sociology. Chicago: Rand McNally.
NEWCOMB, T. M. (1953) "An approach to the study of communicative acts." Psych. Rev. 60 (November): 393-404.
RILEY, M. W. and S. H. FLOWERMAN (1951) "Group relations as a variable in communications research." Amer. Soc. Rev. 16 (April): 174-180.
RILEY, M. W. and J. W. RILEY, Jr. (1951) "A sociological approach to communications research." Public Opinion Q. 15 (Fall): 444-460.
ROBINSON, J. P. (1969) "Television and leisure time: yesterday, today, and (maybe) tomorrow." Public Opinion Q. 33 (Summer): 210-222.
--- and P. M. HIRSCH (1969) "It's the sound that does it." Psychology Today 3 (October): 42-45.
ROSEN, B. C. (1955-1956) "The reference group approach to the parental factor in attitude and behavior formation." Social Forces 34 (December): 137-144.
--- (1955) "Conflicting group membership: a study of parent-peer group cross pressures." Amer. Soc. Rev. 20 (April): 155-161.
ROSZAK, T. (1969) The Making of a Counter Culture. New York: Doubleday.
STEINER, G. A. (1963) The People Look at Television. New York: Alfred A. Knopf.
WALLACH, M. A. (1964) "Art, science and representation: toward an experimental psychology of aesthetics," pp. 412-426 in R. J. C. Harper, C. C. Anderson, C. M. Christensen, and S. M. Hunka (eds.) The Cognitive Processes: Readings. Englewood Cliffs: Prentice-Hall.
WATZLAWICK, P., H. H. BEAVIN, and D. D. JACKSON (1967) Pragmatics of Human Communication. New York: W. W. Norton.
WOLFE, T. (1968) The Pump House Gang. New York: Bantam.

Sociological Approaches to the Pop Music Phenomenon

PAUL M. HIRSCH
University of Chicago

Social scientists have long theorized about "mass society" and "mass culture" and, generally, are appalled by the frightening images brought to mind by these concepts. A wide-ranging debate over their validity, a concern about the "functions" of the mass media in modern society, and their "effects" on the general public have been major subjects of mass communications research for the last two decades.[1] Studies of popular entertainment too often are based exclusively on these concerns.

American mass entertainment has undergone an extraordinary set of transformations in recent years. Several revolutions in communications technology, shifts in program content, altered audience composition, and public opinion have received widespread attention. A related transformation, less widely discussed, has occurred in the *organization* of mass entertainment. Today's entertainment industries bear little resemblance to their namesakes of twenty years ago.

This paper will discuss four sociological approaches to the study of popular culture and relate each to a set of radical changes that have

---

Author's Note: *This paper was part of an ongoing study of changing popular song styles, adolescents' musical taste preferences, and the structure of the pop music industry conducted at the Survey Research Center, University*

occurred in American popular music since the early 1950s. I will argue that the fragmented and disordered state of systematic research in this area is at least partly due to the failure of sociologists to integrate these several approaches; and that an adequate understanding of our changing popular culture in general–and of the "rock revolution" in particular–will require studies of the organization of the industries involved, the impact of technological change upon their output, as well as studies of their content and sociological and psychological effects. In the sections to follow, we will examine briefly (1) content analyses and the functional approach to the mass media, (2) the impact of popular music on its audience, (3) the impact of technological change on mass media programming, and (4) organizational analysis of entertainment industries.

CONTENT ANALYSES AND THE FUNCTIONAL APPROACH TO THE MASS MEDIA

The content of mass media programming has been analyzed periodically in professional journals since the early 1940s. Whatever the medium, be it magazine stories (Johns-Heine and Gerth, 1949; Berelson and Salter, 1946), movie themes (Kracauer, 1949; Wolfenstein and Leites, 1950), popular songs, television serials (Arnheim, 1949), or comic strips (Auster, 1954), a single conclusion has emerged consistently: controversial subjects are avoided, and an idealized set of traditional values are reinforced.

Popular songs produced by Tin Pan Alley have always been notorious for their single-minded devotion to lyrics about "moon and June," to the virtual exclusion of all other topics. In 1944, Peatman reported that practically all popular tunes fell into three categories: "happy in love," "sad in love," and "novelty songs with sex interest." In 1957, Horton found that song lyrics had changed very little since the earlier study. Eighty-seven percent of popular song lyrics still pertained to the "drama of courtship" (Horton, 1957). The remaining thirteen percent:

---

of Michigan, under the direction of Dr. Stephen B. Withey. I wish to thank Dr. John Robinson for generously permitting me to paraphrase our joint research and Dr. Withey for comments on an earlier version of this paper, presented at the 1970 meetings of the International Communications Association. Funds for this project were provided by NIMH Grant 1 RO 1 MH17064-01.

> range widely and show no clear-cut focus. They include song dances, general narrative ballads on love themes, religious songs, comic songs, and others that could not be classified [Carey, 1969: 730].

These findings bore out Hayakawa's (1955) critique in "Popular Songs Versus the Facts of Life" and supported the sociological consensus that mass entertainment and mass media programming serve to reinforce conventional morality, play a small role in motivating individuals toward organized social action, and present their audiences with a continuous flow of standardized trivia. Many critics have condemned such programming for failing to educate or uplift its followers or for encouraging escapism and a form of false consciousness. Others have defended it as harmless in its effects and democratic in providing audiences with the entertainment which ratings and box office receipts have shown they like best.[2]

The Changing American Popular Song

Until recently, a single conclusion on which nearly all observers *could* agree, based on their content analyses of mass media programs, was that popular culture supports prevailing norms, that it is either an agent of social control or epiphenomenal in its impact. This conclusion has been challenged increasingly since the early 1960s. Movie themes (Gans, 1964), large-circulation magazine articles and stories (Brown, 1968; Friedrich, 1969), and, in particular, popular song lyrics can no longer be said, without substantial qualification, to either (a) reflect the dominant values of American society or (b) direct their appeal to the broadest markets available–i.e., to what is generally called the "lowest common denominator." By 1966, only seventy percent of popular song hits concerned stages in the courtship process (Carey, 1969). The remaining songs' lyrics reveal more specific concerns: the role of the individual in the conventional world has become a crucial issue. "Will he become part of the conventional world or will he drop out and create his own scene? The decision to do something about one's life, to think for one's self, no matter what the consequences, is generally enjoined" (Carey, 1969: 730).

"Social Protest" Hits

More specifically, a rising proportion of best-selling popular songs contain lyrics that comment on controversial subjects previously avoided by songwriters. Increasingly, song lyrics have come to call Establishment norms into question and, implicitly or explicitly, to sanction alternative courses of action. (This shift in content has been demonstrated by Carey, 1969; Mooney, 1968; Cole, 1970; Peterson and Berger, 1967; and McLaughlin, 1968.) Whereas Horton (1957) found only thirteen percent of popular songs unrelated to courtship patterns, Carey reported, in 1969, that the proportion had more than doubled to thirty percent. Many of these hit songs contained lyrics which condemned war, acknowledged drug use, or otherwise challenged the status quo. The pattern of courtship, idealized in the remaining seventy percent, is no longer one to which a majority of adults would likely subscribe (e.g., it is more physical, less romantic, less permanent).

A number of writers (Robinson and Hirsch, 1969a, and 1969b; Denisoff and Levine, 1969; and Cole, 1970) have categorized as social protest all hit songs whose lyrics are concerned with controversial themes surrounding the morality of war, relations between different racial groups, drug usage, and also any songs whose lyrics are critical of widely accepted values or legitimized roles in American society. Several examples of popular songs with social protest lyrics are:

Itemize the things you covet
As you squander through your life,
Bigger cars, bigger houses,
Term insurance for your wife,
Tuesday evenings with your harlot
And on Wednesdays it's your charlatan analyst
He's high up on your list
You better take care of business, Mr. Businessman.

[*Mr. Businessman* recorded by Ray Stevens] [3]

Yes it's true I am a young man
But I'm old enough to kill
I don't want to kill nobody
But I must if you so will
All I know is that I'm young
And your rules, they are old
If I've got to kill to live
Then there's something left untold
It's the rules, not the soldiers
That are my real enemy
2 + 2 in on my mind.

[*2 + 2* recorded by Bob Seger] [4]

Leave your cares behind
Come with us and find
The pleasures of a journey to the center
of the mind

But please realize you'll probably be
surprised
For it's a land unknown to man
Where fantasy is fact
So if you can please understand
You might not come back
Take a ride to the land inside and you'll see
How happy life could be.

[Journey to the Center of the Mind
recorded by the Amboy Dukes] [5]

Listen to the children while they play,
Now ain't it kind of funny what the children say,
Cheat on your taxes, don't be a fool,
Now what was that you said about a golden rule?
Never mind the rule, just play to win
And hate your neighbor for the shade of his skin,
Stab him in the back is the name of the game,
And mommy and daddy are who's to blame,
Skip a rope.

[Skip a Rope recorded by Hensen Cargill] [6]

Hit protest songs such as these, which hurl challenges at conventional political and moral beliefs, have engendered strong reactions, much like the public outcry that has greeted a number of X-rated motion pictures. Most recently, for example, Art Linkletter, after testifying before a congressional committee on drug abuse, singled out the popular music industry for encouraging youngsters to experiment with illegal drugs:

> Almost every time a top-40 record is played on the radio, it is an ad for acid, marijuana, and trips. The lyrics of the popular songs and the jackets on the albums . . . are all a complete, total campaign for the fun and thrill of trips [New York Times, 1969].

In May 1967, *Billboard* magazine reported that Gordon McClendon, president of a chain of (nonrock) radio and television stations, had instituted a panel of "prostitutes, ex-prostitutes, junkies, and ex-junkies to assist in weeding out suggestive records . . . in his campaign against 'filth' in the record industry." He stated:

> We've had all we can stand of the record industry's glorifying marijuana, LSD, and sexual activity. The newest Beatles record has a line of 40,000 purple hearts in one arm. Is that what you want your children to listen to? . . . [I call for] a rather updated version of the Boston Tea Party. I suppose you might

> call it the Wax Party—one in which all the distasteful records which deal with sex, sin, and drugs [would be purged from radio air-play].

It should be noted the Top 40 stations generally boycotted the Beatles' record referred to by McClendon, and, by any reasonable standard, Linkletter exaggerated strongly the extent to which records aired by Top 40 stations contain references to drugs. It is equally clear, however, that a significant change *has* taken place in American popular music: unconventional messages about sex, drugs, and politics are recorded routinely now by major record companies and disseminated by widely listened-to radio stations across the land. Few would have predicted this development as recently as 1960. In an era of "message" films and "progressive rock," movies, popular records, and radio broadcasting no longer can be characterized in functional terms simply as escapist agents of social control. Today, this description is better illustrated by the programming of commerical television networks.

Theories about the social functions served by the media are rooted empirically in analyses of mass media articles and program content. A shift in the direction of the messages transmitted is assumed to induce, or reflect, attitudinal changes on the part of the audience. One inference drawn readily from content analyses is that the themes abstracted by the researcher are the same ones perceived by the audience. A typical example of this inferential leap appears in Carey's article (1969: 722), where, despite admirable qualifications elsewhere in the text, it is suggested that observed changes in content signify, a priori, a "dramatic shift in the value preferences of young people." That this inference may not be justified is a general finding of investigators working in the second traditional approach to mass communications research, students of the impact, or the effects, of the mass media on the general population.

THE IMPACT OF POPULAR MUSIC ON ITS AUDIENCE

Many analysts and observers of the popular music scene seem to subscribe to all or part of a "hypodermic needle" theory of song lyrics' effects. It is assumed that (implied or explicit) values expressed in popular hit protest songs are (a) clear to a majority of listeners, (b) subscribed to by a large proportion of listeners, and (c) likely to influence the attitudes and behavior of the uncommitted. The theory further assumes a "direct hit" for messages broadcast by the electronic media and directed at an undifferentiated target audience. None of these assumptions has ever been tested empirically: Are song lyrics purely epiphenomenal, or can they be taken as reliable indicators or determinants of teenagers' values?

The hypodermic needle theory has persisted despite the finding of Katz and Lazarsfeld (1955) and others that seemingly straightforward information is perceived differently by individual receptors, for whom it is filtered and interpreted by opinion leaders and informal associates. In the case of rock-and-roll songs, the message contained in the lyrics frequently is obscure, rather than straightforward. Lyrics, generally, are treated by performers as but one of several components of the total sound. Consequently, they must be abstracted from accompanying complex vocal and instrumental arrangements (which often tend to drown out the words) by a special effort on the part of the listener. Once the lyrics are deciphered, their meaning may appear ambiguous or confusing. Teenagers may not impute the same meanings to a song's words as do social researchers and critics. As we shall see, they tend to be unaware of many songs' lyrics and messages: Most teenagers are attracted to popular records more by their overall sound and beat—or the performing group—than by their verbal content (Robinson and Hirsch, 1969a, 1969b). Systematic social research has yet to demonstrate any effects of popular song lyrics upon their listeners.

Beyond the number of copies a record sells and the age groups to which it appeals, there is very little published information available about record consumers. We do know that the median age of consumers of hit singles has been decreasing steadily since the early 1950s, hence it is very probable that the audience for popular music today is younger than its counterpart of fifteen or more years ago (New York Times, 1967; Record Industry Association of America, 1964). Studies of Americans' musical taste also have found that favorite types of music and social background are highly associated (Schuessler, 1948; Coleman, 1961; Brunswick, 1962). But sociologists only recently have begun to investigate questions such as: Are all Top 40 records purchased by the same population, or do certain popular song styles appeal disproportionately to particular groups? Are records containing deviant messages primarily purchased for the content of their lyrics, or is it the sound and beat of the rendition that appeals to their buyers? How closely can musical taste preferences be predicted from a knowledge of background variables?

Findings by Robinson and Hirsch

Several studies of tenagers' song style preferences have been conducted by Robinson and Hirsch to get at preliminary answers to these questions.

Four surveys of high school students in Michigan were completed under Robinson's direction, and two national samples are in the analysis stage. Between Fall 1967 and Winter 1969, approximately 1,200 high school students in Detroit, Flint, and Grand Rapids, Michigan, filled out a confidential questionnaire on their attitudes toward popular songs in general and current popular social protest hist in particular. A number of surprises emerged from these data. Findings from the first two Michigan surveys were reported in detail by Robinson and Hirsch (1969a). In brief, these included:

(1) The universal popularity of "current popular hits" across the entire sample. Only one percent expressed a dislike for popular hits. In this sense, teenagers do constitute a "homogeneous" audience for this type of music.

(2) Each respondent was asked to list his "three favorite records." These were coded into one of four "song style" categories: "rhythm and blues (soul) hits," "social protest hits," "other hits," and "square." All named songs on the popular record "charts" were coded into one of the first three categories. Any record named which was never on the hit parade was placed in the residual, "square" category. Ninety-three percent of all records listed were popular song hits.

Respondents' song style preferences within the category "current popular hits" were found to vary markedly by race and social class. Students listing "protest hits" were disproportionately (2 : 1) from white middle-class homes; students listing "other hits" were disproportionately (2 : 1) from white lower-class backgrounds; and teenagers listing "rhythm and blues hits" were overwhelmingly Negro (8 : 1). Age, sex, grades in school, and number of friends enumerated failed to predict well the popular song style preference. There was little overlap or crossover of song style preferences among the three records listed by each respondent.

(3) Fewer than thirty percent were able to write out correctly the "message" allegedly contained in four controversial hit "protest" song lyrics. Our coding of "correct interpretations" was based primarily on the explanation of a given song's meaning presented in the popular press. For example, we coded any reference to "LSD" as "correct" for the song, "*L*ucy in the *S*ky with *D*iamonds," on the basis of widely circulated accounts in the press that this was its "message"; a denial by the Beatles that this was their intent was thus ignored. In some instances we took what *we* considered an obvious interpretation as the "correct" one (e.g., our coding of the

song, "Mr. Businessman," cited earlier, as a social protest hit. For further discussion of the songs selected and coding procedures employed in defining "messages" and song styles, see Robinson and Hirsch (1969a).

Correct interpretations ranged from ten to thirty percent, depending on the particular song in question. A "selective listening" phenomenon was noted, wherein many students appear unaware of certain songs played over their favorite radio station–they are "tuned in" only to selections in the style with which their background characteristics are associated. In place of the expected lowest common denominator (homogeneous) audience, we found the audience heterogeneous, stratified by social class and song style preference. When asked directly if a song's attraction lies in its sound or its meaning seventy percent responded that they are more attracted by a song's sound. These data strongly suggest that a majority of teenagers fail to perceive the "deviant" messages contained in a number of hit social protest songs.

Thus, while nearly all teenagers followed current popular hits, there was much patterned variation *within* this musical category. Listeners to Top 40 radio stations did not constitute a single audience. Rather, the composite audience broke down into stratified social groups, each of which listened selectively for the air-play of the popular song style with which it was associated. To generalize from our surveys, we will assume that these findings (a) are not specific to two cities in the Midwest; (b) would be replicated in smaples of persons over 17 years of age; and (c) have not been affected significantly by the introduction of "progressive rock" formats by FM radio stations in most major cities. (We are presently testing each of these assumptions with data from two national samples).

If certain popular song styles appeal disproportionately to particular subgroups within the American teenage population, it follows that *all* Top 40 or rock-and-roll records are not interchangeable in the eyes of young consumers. The stratified teenage audience (usually viewed by adults as an undifferentiated horde) is an aggregate of individuals who form distinct popular music subaudiences–for protest hits, *or* other hits, *or* rhythm and blues hits–with little crossover in membership. As radio station formats become more specialized, each subaudience is turning to speciality programming that features just one popular music style, rather than the more usual Top 40 potpourri. Thus, progressive rock stations, featuring primarily what we have labeled "protest hits," have drawn their audience almost exclusively from well-to-do high school and college students who formerly listened to all-purpose Top 40 stations. Blacks attend to soul-formatted rather than Top 40 stations whenever a choice is available (Robinson and Hirsch, 1969b); and white Southern teenagers probably are disproportionately receptive to all-country stations. The Top 40 format, still featuring the something-for-everyone-in-the-pop-music audience formula, thus, faces increasing competition. Paradoxically, this will encourage cultural pluralism in the aggregate but, simultaneously, will increase the cultural isolation of each audience subculture.

We have, so far, examined two sociological approaches to the study of popular music in the United States. First, the content analysis approach showed that popular song lyrics have changed radically during the last fifteen years. However, our second approach to the pop music phenomenon—the study of songs' impact on listeners and consumers—suggested that caution be exercised before attributing too much of the change in musical message content to a dramatic shift in the values of young people. We saw, for example, that the vast majority of teenagers sampled in two Michigan cities, including those attracted by the social protest song style, were unable to interpret the messages these records allegedly contained in the same terms as research scholars and social critics. That is, most teenagers made no reference to drugs, sex, or politics when asked to interpret the meanings of songs which *we* believed said a great deal about each of these subjects (Robinson and Hirsch, 1969b).

A third and fourth approach to the study of popular culture provide a new perspective which should aid in explaining the changes observed in popular music.

THE IMPACT OF TECHNOLOGICAL CHANGE ON MASS MEDIA CONTENT

As each new technologically advanced mass medium appears, it tends to take over the functions served by an earlier medium, forcing the latter to redefine its role. This is essentially what happened to radio with the advent of television. The resultant competition that developed between them threatened radio's existence to such an extent that it had to seek new and different markets which could complement those of television. The movie industry was affected similarly. Radio and movie formats have since undergone a series of rapid changes in their attempts to maintain an audience in the face of television's better capacity to provide superior mass entertainment.

Rock-and-roll radio emerged in the fifties as part of the radio industry's confused response to the onslaught of television. Network programming, directed at the largest possible cross-section of listeners, was replaced by formats directed at subcultural markets–i.e., small aggregates of listeners previously neglected because their numbers could not equal the size required by the logic of network programming (Gans, 1961; Hirsch, 1969). *All*-news, *all*-country, *all*-Top 40, *all*-soul, and *all*-underground stations are each a successful illustration of this strategy of slicing up the total radio audience into subcultural groupings interested in a single specialty broadcast format. Movies adopted a similar strategy when they opted for problem films (Gans, 1964): the hitherto cross-sectional mass audience was divided into its constituent parts.

American youth, thus, was provided a medium all its own as the accidental by-product of a revolution in communications technology and its economic consequences. The age structure of our population encouraged special programming directed at the youth audience. Young people became increasingly numerous and prosperous at the same time that radio was forced into subcultural markets. The postwar baby boom was growing up and represented substantial purchasing power ($10 billion by 1959; over $25 billion today). Top 40 radio was tried on an experimental basis and proved to be highly successful.

The Top 40 Format

The Top 40 format combines all popular song styles and continuously broadcasts a repetitive selection of thirty to forty records per week. Most of these are played for several weeks before being dropped from the playlist. A limited number of soul, country, protest, oldie, and other hits are thrown together into a preset mix, which is designed to include something for everyone in the mass audience for popular music. Top 40 hit records are identifiable very often only by their common characteristic of having all been selected (somewhat arbitrarily) for air-play by Top 40 radio station programmers.

For example, performers like the Beatles or the Rolling Stones are associated directly with the term "rock-and-roll" because their records were heard first over Top 40 radio stations. Other singers' records often obtain air-play initially from non-Top 40 programs but are "coopted" onto the Top 40 playlist at a later date and thus exposed to the larger mass audience. Upon the selection of his record(s) by Top 40 stations, a singer is transformed overnight from a relative unknown into a "rock star."

Performers whose records have "crossed over" in this fashion include the late Janis Joplin, Bob Dylan, James Brown, Country Joe and the Fish, and–earlier in her career–Barbra Streisand. Since all records selected by Top 40 station program directors are thereby conferred the status of rock records the musical style sometimes cannot be defined independently of the radio stations over which the records are broadcast.

This observation applies equally well to the music industry's definition of "underground" popular hits. A growing number of records broadcast by radio stations featuring the "progressive rock" format appear to be unconcerned with political questions, drug usage, or other controversial issues. If a record is *played* first by an underground station, however, it is generally defined as underground throughout the industry–regardless of its message content–perhaps because it was found to appeal first to the underground audience.

The ascendance of television had a further impact on popular music. In record industry parlance, "air-play is the lifeline of any company." Before the widespread adoption of television, four major record companies sold 75% of all hit records in the United States (Peterson and Berger, 1967). Their output was geared almost entirely to the program choices of network radio. When radio stations switched to subcultural programming, this "Big Four" were taken by surprise; they were unskilled at recording the musical styles that had been delegated for years to small entrepreneurs who catered primarily to the smaller subcultural markets.

Unanticipated Consequences

This brief overview of the impact of technological change on programming decisions in the mass media represents a third sociological approach to the study of popular culture. The widespread adoption of television, and the manner in which licenses were granted, led to a set of unanticipated consequences, of which rock-and-roll is but one example. This approach derives from the teachings of Merton (1936) and Ogburn (1964), whose perspectives on the analysis of social change should sensitize more sociologists to seek out unanticipated consequences of this type. In the present case, it is very doubtful that popular music could have changed as radically as we have seen were it not for the structural changes wrought by seemingly unrelated developments in mass communications technology.

The impact of technological change is closely associated with the fourth and last approach we will examine to the study of mass entertainment: the study of entertainment industries as organization sets.

ORGANIZATIONAL ANALYSIS OF ENTERTAINMENT INDUSTRIES

The advent of the Top 40 radio format, and the instant popularity of the records it featured, fundamentally altered the character of the market at which pop records were directed. Long used to producing popular music for the mainstream American audience, the largest record companies were unable and, at first, unwilling to plunge into subcultural recording and marketing. A resultant vacuum was filled by eager small entrepreneurs. Singles (45 r.p.m.) cost only several hundred dollars to record *and* manufacture (Hirsch, 1969); the prospect of huge returns on such a small investment in a highly uncertain environment resulted in the establishment of many new record companies and a rise in the industry's output to over 300 new singles *per week.* Large record firms had not yet developed the type of personnel required to record the raucous sounds of rock-and-roll music. At first, they simply served as national distributers for rock records manufactured by smaller competitors.

All record companies were forced now to compete to an unprecedented degree for the exclusive right to record pop musicians and entertainers whose records were most likely to receive air-play. At the height of this free-for-all, in 1958, the "payola" scandals brought to light the fact that record companies were bribing radio station personnel to insure air-play for their new releases.

The organization and direction of American popular music were also affected by the outcome of a suit against the American Society of Composers, Authors, and Publishers (ASCAP) in 1941. Small entrepreneurs, songwriters, and musicians were aided considerably in their attempt to break into the recording field by a judgment striking down ASCAP's legal right to prevent the recording and broadcasting of songs composed by nonmember writers. Membership admissions had been restrictive and discriminatory (Mooney, 1968).

In order to retain sales leadership and to capture subcultural markets from increasingly aggressive competitors, the large record companies were forced to (1) purchase the contracts of up-and-coming artists from smaller companies (this is how Elvis Presley became associated with RCA Records, for example), and, more importantly, (2) undertake negotiations with the musicians and record producers, who were in an increasingly advantageous bargaining position vis-à-vis the record companies: (a) rock-and-roll tunes, unlike earlier popular songs, are composed generally by the same musicians who record them, hence it became more difficult for companies to select the songs to be recorded by the musicians; (b) the entry of more companies into this field created a "seller's market" (Gleason, 1969). *The net result of these events within the industry was that performers were able to obtain an increasing amount of artistic control over the songs which they recorded and which were released by major record companies.*

Many analysts attribute the daring and radical lyrics of some of today's hit songs to the desire of record companies to please, or to convert, their consumers. Scholars in the content analysis tradition and social critics tend to believe that the controversial lyrics of some current songs reflect or influence the attitudes of an overwhelming majority of young people. Much more attention should be focused on the companies' losses in bargaining power vis-à-vis the musicians and on the large-scale intrusion of *musicians'* values into the songs they record. Carey (1969: 723) reports that by 1966,

> slightly over 65 percent of the songs (containing lyrics expressing the "new (protest) values" were written by members of the group which recorded them. Lyrics which are not rock and roll, those celebrating older, more conventional values, were characteristically not written by the groups which recorded them. Only 13 percent of this type of lyrics were written by the groups which sang them.

The intrusion of a new set of values into popular songs composed by the groups which record and perform them is clear from the content analyses reviewed earlier. It seems equally clear, however, that a majority of teenage listeners and consumers are unaware of the messages conveyed by these songs and are generally indifferent (Robinson and Hirsch, 1969a, 1969b; Denisoff and Levine, 1969). The most plausible explanation for the value change in popular song lyrics is that changes in the organization of the music industry, mainly the demise of network radio, expanding markets, and an increase in the number of competing record companies enabled musicians to obtain the power to decide the content of the songs they would record.

The Rise of "Progressive Rock"

A long-standing tradition of industry self-censorship suffered perhaps its greatest defeat in the scramble for "psychedelic" recording artists during the early months of 1967. Once every major record company jumped on the momentary bandwagon to sign popular local bands in San Francisco to recording contracts, a seller's market developed. Unprecedented cash advances of up to $65,000 to performing groups were reported by music critic Ralph Gleason (1969). Columbia Records reportedly invested $250,000 simply to purchase the recording contract of Janis Joplin's group, Big Brother and the Holding Company, from another firm (Gleason, 1969). As the number of ex-folk and jazz musicians following their colleagues Bob Dylan, Simon and Garfunkel, and the Byrds into the world of rock music increased, the definition of what is permissible in the content of popular song lyrics broadened significantly. Whereas record companies formerly could dictate the material to be recorded by musicians under contract, they were now in the relatively powerless position of having to approve or veto material already recorded and available for mass distribution.

Once they had invested in these groups, the record companies undertook an extensive marketing campaign to realize a healthy return on their investment (Hirsch, 1969). Unexpected resistance was encountered initially, however, from Top 40 radio stations' program directors and retail record dealers. Retailers hesitated to order records by unknown groups unless they could be made familiar to consumers via air-play over local Top 40 stations. But program directors in many parts of the country viewed the "San Francisco sound" as unproven in its appeal to audiences outside of the West Coast and hesitated to add new records in this popular song style to their playlists. The problem of air-play was solved at this point by the adoption of the progressive rock format by FM stations in major cities across the country. This format, as it features primarily hit protest songs, appeals predominantly to upper-middle-class white teenagers and young adults. Most treatments of rock music in the popular press seem directed at these children's parents. They create a false impression in equating protest hits (one of several distinct popular song styles) with *all* popular hits and in confusing the class-based audience for protest hits with the total youth audience. Each of these inferences, as we have seen, is unwarranted and misleading. While we have located several youth subcultures insofar as popular song style preferences are concerned, we found no evidence for the existence of a single, unified teenage culture strong enough to overcome within-group class and racial differences.

CONCLUSION

This paper reviewed four sociological approaches to the study of popular culture and related each to changes in the content of popular song lyrics during the last twenty years. We examined the method of content analysis, the search for effects, the impact of technological change on mass media programming, and some consequences of organizational changes in an entertainment industry. The latter two perspectives help to explain the paradoxical research finding of radical changes in song lyrics, on the one hand, and the apparent indifference of the teenage audience toward all song meanings, on the other.

Conventional courtship themes in popular song lyrics have given way to less traditional messages about all areas of social life. This change is partly due to (a) the ascendance of performers over previously powerful industry censors, and (b) changes in communications technology which transformed the radio industry. There is no evidence that popular songs per se affect the attitudes and behavior of young people nor even that a majority of listeners are aware of what many consider to be the message of hit protest songs.

NOTES

1. Two excellent reviews of the literature and arguments on both sides may be found in Gans (1966) and Brown (1968). See also the excellent collection of essays gathered by Rosenberg and White (1957).

2. Bauer and Bauer (1960) and Gans (1966) present extensive reviews of the critical literature, though both attempt to discredit the critics' arguments (Coser, 1960). For much of the original source material, see the anthologies of Rosenberg and White (1957) and Jacobs (1961).

3. Ahab Publishing Co. (B.M.I.); Monument Records.

4. Gear Publishing Co. (ASCAP); Capital Records.

5. Publisher unknown; Mainstream Records.

6. Tree Publishing Co. (B.M.I.) Monument Records.

7. The image of a hypodermic needle to characterize a theory of powerful, one-way mass media "effects" was first suggested by Berelson et al. (1954).

REFERENCES

ARNHEIM, R. (1943) " The world of the daytime serial," pp. 507-548 in P. Lazarsfeld and F. Stanton (eds.) Radio Research, 1942-1943. New York: Duell, Sloan & Pearce.

AUSTER, D. (1954) "A content analysis of Little Orphan Annie." Social Problems 2: 26-33.

BAUER, R. A. and A. H. BAUER (1960) "American mass society and mass media." J. of Social Issues 16, 3: 3-66.

BERELSON, B. R. and P. SALTER (1946) "An analysis of magazine fiction." Public Opinion Q. 10: 168-197.

BERELSON, B. R., P. LAZARSFELD, and W. McPHEE (1954) Voting. Chicago: Univ. of Chicago Press.

Billboard (1967) "Anti-smut McClendon to set up fringe panel." May 20: 1.

BROWN, R. L. (1968) "The creative process in the popular arts." International Social Science J. 20, 4: 613-624.

BRUNSWICK, A. (1962) "Popular taste in music as reflected by behavior with regard to phonograph records." Unpublished.

CAREY, T. (1969) "Changing courtship patterns in the popular song." Amer. J. of Sociology 74 (May): 720-731.

COLE, R. (1970) "Top songs in the sixties: a content analysis of popular lyrics." Research Division, School of Journalism and Mass Communication, University of Minnesota. (mimeo)

COLEMAN, J. S. (1961) The Adolescent Society. Glencoe: Free Press.

COSER, L. (1960) "Comments on Bauer and Bauer." J. of Social Issues 16, 3: 78-84.

DENISOFF, R. S. and M. H. LEVINE (1969) "The popular protest song: the case of the 'eve of destruction.' " California State College. (working paper)

FRIEDRICH, O. (1969) "Killing the Saturday Evening Post." Harper's 239 (December): 92-121.

GANS, H. L. (1966) "Popular culture in America: social problem in a mass society or social asset in a pluralist society?" pp. 549-620 in H. S. Becker (ed.) Social Problems: A Modern Approach. New York: John Wiley.

--- (1964) "The rise of the problem film." Social Problems 11, 4 (Spring): 327-336.

--- (1961) "Pluralist aesthetics and subcultural programming: a proposal for cultural democracy in the mass media." Studies in Public Communication 3: 28-35.

GLEASON, R. (1969) The Jefferson Airplane and the San Francisco Sound. New York: Ballantine.

HAYAKAWA, S. I. (1955) "Popular songs vs. the facts of life." Etc: A General Review of Semantics 12: 83-95.

HIRSCH, P. (1970) "The processing of fads and fashions by cultural industries: an organization set analysis." Presented at the 1970 Annual Meetings of the American Sociological Association. (mimeo)

--- (1969) The Structure of the Popular Music Industry. Ann Arbor: Survey Research Center, University of Michigan.

HORTON, T. (1957) "The dialogue of courtship in popular songs." Amer. J. of Sociology 62 (May): 569-578.

JACOBS, N. [ed] (n.d.) Culture for the Millions? Boston: Beacon Press.

JOHNS-HEINE, P. and H. H. GERTH (1949) "Values in mass periodical fiction, 1921-1940." Public Opinion Q. 13: 105-113.

KATZ, E. and P. LAZARSFELD (1955) Personal Influence. Glencoe: Free Press.

KRACAUER S. (1949) "National types as Hollywood presents them." Public Opinion Q. 13: 53-72.

LIPSET, S. M. and N. J. SMELSER [eds.] (1961) Sociology: The Progress of a Decade. Englewood Cliffs: Prentice-Hall.

McLAUGHLIN, M.C. (1968) "The social world of American popular songs." Master's thesis, Department of Anthropology, Cornell University.

MERTON, R. K. (1936) "The unanticipated consequences of purposive social action." Amer. Soc. Rev. 1: 894-904.

MOONEY, F. (1968) "Popular music since the 1920's: the significance of shifting taste." Amer. Q. 20: 68-85.

New York Times (1969) "Linkletter talks on drugs to Nixon." October 24: 18.

--- (1967) "Record industry turning to younger producers." September 13: 38.

OGBURN, W. F. (1964) On Culture and Social Change. O. D. Duncan (ed.) Chicago: Univ. of Chicago Press.

PEATMAN, J. (1944) "Radio and popular music," pp. 335-393, in P. Lazarsfeld and F. Stanton (eds.) Radio Research: 1942-1943. New York: Duell, Sloan & Pearce.

PETERSON, A. and D. G. BERGER (1967) "The dollar and pap culture: the influence of changing industry structure on the control of social commentary in popular music." (Unpublished). Record Industry Association of America (1964)

Record Industry Association of America (1964) Radio and Records.

RIESMAN, D. (1954) "Listening to popular music," in B. Rosenberg and D. M. White [eds.] (1957) Mass Culture. Glencoe: Free Press.

ROBINSON, P. and P. M. HIRSCH (1969a) "Teenage response to rock and roll protest songs." Presented at the 1969 Annual Meetings of the American Sociological Association, San Francisco.

--- (1969b) "It's the sound that does it." Psychology Today 3 (October): 42-45.

ROSENBERG, B. and D. M. WHITE [eds.] (1957) Mass Culture. Glencoe: Free Press.

SCHUESSLER, K. (1948) "Social background and musical taste." Amer. Soc. Rev. 13: 330-335.

WOLFE, T. (1967) "The first tycoon of teen," in The Kandy-Kolored Tangerine Flake Streamline Baby. New York: Fauer, Strauss & Giroux.

WOLFENSTEIN, M. and N. LEITES (1950) The Good-Bad Girl in Movies: A Psychological Study. New York: Free Press.

Top Songs in the Sixties

A Content Analysis of Popular Lyrics

RICHARD R. COLE
University of North Carolina

Although several studies have been conducted regarding the mass media and teenagers, relatively little attention has been given to one mass medium that is particularly pertinent to the youth subculture—the popular recording. Teenagers purchase more records than any other age group, and the popular record is a factor in transmitting elements of the youth subculture.

Riesman (1957) asserts that what the teenager receives in the mass media is framed by his perception of the peer groups to which he belongs; these groups not only rate songs but select for their members what is to be "heard" in each tune. One of the most readily discernible influences of popular music is on teenagers' appearance. The Beatles, the most noted singing group of recent years, were of prime import in popularizing current long hair styles of young men; the influence on clothing styles by British groups with "the Carnaby Street look" is equally obvious.

Sebald (1968: 232-233) writes that American youths exhibit special admiration for recording stars, with whom they tend to identify and who represent significant others. Johnstone and Katz (1957) interviewed teenage girls and concluded that preferences in popular music varied according to the neighborhood of residence and to a girl's popularity among her peers.

Adorno (1950: 314) asserts that the favorite songs of popular music fans will be those most often "plugged" on radio. Hirsch (1969: 7, 54) describes a complicated preselection system operating in the highly competitive music industry but concludes that the Top 40 audience hears the records it has the greatest probability of liking because broadcasters tend to choose records for which the public is expressing, or has expressed, a preference.

This preference is for the "total impact" of a record, although systematic analyses have ignored the music in favor of lyrics. Disagreement exists on the significance of lyrics. Robinson and Hirsch (1969) contend that "the vast majority of teenage listeners are unaware of what the lyrics of hit protest songs are about."[1] Hayakawa (1957: 400) notes, however, that popular songs often are memorized and sung in the course of adolescent courtship, and Horton (1957: 577) points out that many times young persons murmur lyrics while dancing. A reasonable conclusion is that even though lyrics are but a portion of a song's total impact, they are an important portion.

Peatman (1944) analyzed lyrics of 90 Hit Parade songs from 1941-1942 and found that only 8% had no sex interest. Horton (1957) examined 235 lyrics published in four periodicals devoted to popular songs and found that love was the central concern in 87% of the lyrics. Carey (1969a) attempted to repeat Horton's analysis by comparing the 1955 lyrics with 227 songs published in 1966 magazines.[2] He concluded that lyrics in the latter period had changed significantly from 1955, the major difference being "the more active character" of the 1966 boy-girl courtship. Carey (1969b) analyzed 176 lyrics thematically, concluding that rock-and-roll songs reflected "new bohemian" values. Of these four studies, Peatman gave the most attention to "popularity" over time by listing the number of weeks songs in his love categories remained on the Hit Parade. The current study attempts to provide a more meaningful criterion for popularity by analyzing leading lyrics throughout a decade, and it includes variables besides love in the analysis.

METHODOLOGY

This study of content analyzes lyrics of the annual Top 10 single songs during each year of the 1960s, based on national popularity ratings by *Billboard* magazine.[3] Of the 100 songs, 7 were instrumentals, giving a total of 93 lyrics for analysis.[4] Two persons coded each of the lyrics.[5]

The general mood of the song as a whole was described as "happy"–expressing pleasure or contentment; "unhappy"–expressing sadness or anxiety; or "balanced"–expressing neither happiness nor unhappiness.

Particular attention was paid to four selected topics, chosen not only because of their currency but also because of their relevance to the youth subculture:

Love-sex: Smith (1962: 5) writes that sex is the most salient variable in fusing the youth subculture. In this study, love-sex was defined generally as concerning romance or physical desire, referring to the overall boy-girl relationship. Five dimensions of love-sex were examined: the relationship, determination of the relationship, dominant participant, predominant type of love, and attitude toward romantic love and physical love.

Religion: Debate in the mass media over the role of religion prompted including this topic in the analysis, although it was expected that references to religion would not be numerous.

Violence: Most of the controversy over violence and the mass media concerns possible effects of violent content on the young, but this author found no scientific investigation of the violent content of popular songs. Gerson's (1968) typology of violence (physical, manipulation of others, and verbal) was used.

Social protest: It was expected that recent songs would manifest more references to social protest–defined as disapproval of situations existing in society or of attitudes widely held or approval of attitudes not held–widely e.g., a protest against war or approval of illegal drugs.

RESULTS

The annual Top 10 songs in the 1960s demonstrated a dramatic shift from the single vocalist, usually male, in the first half of the decade, to the vocal group, usually male also, in the latter half. Single male vocalists sang 53% of the lyrics in 1960-1964 compared to 21% in 1965-1969.

GENERAL MOOD

Over the entire 10 years, more of the 93 songs were unhappy (44%) than happy (39%). The combination of unhappy and balanced lyrics for the decade was 61%. This lack of preference for happy songs became more pronounced in the second half of the decade, increasing from 55% in 1960-1964 to 67% in 1965-1969; the difference, however, was due to an increase in the number of balanced songs rather than an increase in the number of unhappy ones.

Love-sex was the predominant theme in 71% of the lyrics over the decade but in 1965-1969 there were 12% fewer songs in this category than occurred in 1960-1964. Other predominant themes were similar in 1960-1964 and 1965-1969, except for social protest, which accounted for 10% of the lyrics in the second period and none in the first. Few songs were concerned primarily with religion or violence. Songs in the "other" category differed greatly in the two periods. The first five years, in which dancing was the predominant theme of five songs, reflected the popularity of such crazes as the "twist," "pony," and "mashed potato." Half of the 10 other songs in the second period evidenced a thread of personal problems: a youth bemoaned his general discontent—"I can't get no satisfaction," and a girl advised lonely persons to lose themselves in the bright lights of "Downtown." Other lyrics expressed hopelessness and an inability to stand alone.

The analysis indicated that love was a somewhat precarious undertaking that might likely result in resignation to its torments if not in broken hearts. Of the 66 songs in the decade with love-sex as a predominant theme, only 33% were happy, whereas 53% were unhappy, and 14% balanced. Taken together, unhappy and balanced lyrics, as opposed to happy ones, increased from 64% in the first 5 years to 68% in the second period. This paucity of happiness is reasonable considering the fragile and transitory nature of teenage romance.

Males sang approximately 80% of the love-sex songs, and attitudes they expressed toward current sweethearts varied widely. One depressed youth feared for his masculinity because a girl mistreated him:

I've got to stand tall
You know a man can't crawl
For when he knows you tell lies
And he lets them pass by
Then he's not a man at all

[*Cathy's Clown* (1960) recorded by Everly Brothers] [6]

But a profound loss brought another male to tears:

Oh no it can't be teardrops
For a man ain't supposed to cry

[*Raindrops* (1961) recorded by Dee Clark] [7]

In general, the emotions depended on the five love-sex dimensions:

Stage of the relationship: On the whole, the lyrics depicted love as an elusive quarry; participants tended to be either seeking love or involved in the breakup of an unsuccessful relationship. The prologue, concerned with a longing or a search for love, and the breakup stage each accounted for 26% of the lyrics. In the prologue, the typical plaint was:

> I need love, love to ease my mind
> I need to find, find someone to call mine
>
> [*You Can't Hurry Love* (1966) recorded by the Supremes] [8]

In no case was the breakup stage mutually satisfactory to both participants; one person always remained unhappy.

The happy stage, next in frequency, accounted for 23% of the lyrics. During this blissful phase, time often was not a concern ("true love means waiting"), and participants sometimes glossed over faults of their lovers, as when a girl praised her admittedly imperfect boyfriend:

> No handsome face could ever take the place of my guy
> He may not be a movie star but when it comes to being happy we are
>
> [*My Guy* (1964) recorded by Mary Wells] [9]

Frequently, the bliss proved to be short-lived, however, for the downward course of the relationship was depicted in 14% of the lyrics. Here, unlike the happy stage, time was endless:

> They say that time heals a broken heart
> But time stood still since we've been apart
>
> [*I Can't Stop Loving You* (1962) recorded by Ray Charles] [10]

The isolation stage occurred in only 5% of the lyrics, all sung by males. For example:

> I've been in love so many times I thought I knew the score
> But now you've treated me so wrong I can't take any more
> And it looks like I'll never fall in love again
>
> [*I'll Never Fall in Love Again* (1969) recorded by Tom Jones] [11]

The two five-year periods differed in the frequency of stages. Three times as many lyrics in 1960-1964 as in 1965-1969 concerned the breakup phase, and the second period exhibited a marked increase (34% compared with 18%) in the number of prologues described. During the entire ten years, marriage was mentioned in only four lyrics, twice in each period. The great majority of songs were concerned with establishing, continuing, or terminating a nonmarital relationship.

Determination of love: The participants, more than fate, determined the course of relationships in 70% of the songs. Individuals attempted to rise from poverty and from despair. Love-sex was more in the hands of fate than the participants in 15% of the lyrics. A typical reference was, "No matter how they toss the dice, it has to be." Determination by fate rather than by participants rose from 12% in 1960-1964 to 19% in 1965-1969.

Dominant participant: More girls (42%) than boys (15%) dominated love relationships, but this was, in part, a function of the prevalent pattern of male vocalists singing balanced or unhappy lyrics. It was evident, however, that control by one participant was the trend; domination by either boy or girl, taken together, accounted for 58% of the relationships, wheras about equal control by the sexes accounted for only 6%. Feminine domination was more evident in lyrics of the second five-year period (56%) than in the earlier one (29%). Females kept boyfriends awake ("I kept on tossin' and turnin' . . . all night") and toyed with them:

> When you snap your fingers or wink your eye I come
> a-running to you
>
> [*I Can't Help Myself* (1965) recorded by The Four Tops] [12]

Predominant type of love: As expected, romance (71%) as opposed to physical desire (14%) was the predominant type of love throughout the decade. Although the proportion of songs dealing with the two types of love varied no more than 5% between 1960-1964 and 1965-1969, more subtle changes were apparent. Especially in the early years, lyrics tended to evoke a schoolboy tenderness:

> Roses are red, my love, violets are blue
> Sugar is sweet, my love, but not as sweet as you
>
> [*Roses are Red, Violets are Blue* (1962) recorded by Bobby Vinton] [13]

In later years this tended to give way to a more straightforward approach. One boy sang:

First time that I saw you, girl
I knew that I just had to make you mine

[*Dizzy* (1969) recorded by Tommy Row] [14]

General attitudes toward romantic and physical love: The general attitude toward romance in love was nearly all positive over the entire period. From 1960-1964 to 1965-1969, positive attitudes toward romance decreased by 13%. Although most lyrics made no overt statement concerning sexual desire, 23% demonstrated a positive attitude toward it. Several assertions, even in the early years, might be termed suggestive ("Ours, a love I held tightly, feeling the rapture grow, like a flame burning brightly"[15] and "I've got this burning burning yearning feeling inside me, ooh / Deep inside me and it hurts so bad"[16]). But the most striking difference in attitudes toward physical love over the decade appeared to be the more graphic sexual references in later years. The 1960 plea by Elvis Presley:

Your lips excite me, let your arms invite me
For who knows when we'll meet again this way
It's now or never, my love won't wait

[*It's Now or Never*] [17]

was a far cry from the 1968 line by the Cream, a male group, anticipating a visit with a girl:

I'll stay with you till my seeds are dried up

[*Sunshine of Your Love*] [18]

The fourth-ranked song in 1969, *Honky Tonk Women* by the Rolling Stones,[19] spoke matter-of-factly of sexual gratification:

I met a gin-salt bar-room queen in Memphis
She tried to take me upstairs for a ride

And later in the lyric:

I laid a divorcee in New York City

Religion

As expected, few religious references appeared in the lyrics. Religion was the predominant theme of only two songs, both of which manifested positive attitudes toward sacred things. Of the nine other lyrics with any religious assertion, seven demonstrated positive attitudes–including such phrases as a youth's saying "May God bless you" to his girlfriend, and another boy's giving thanks for being alive because "at long last love has arrived." The two negative references toward religion appeared in 1965-1969. Overall, only 12% of the lyrics contained any reference to religion.

Violence

Surprisingly few lyrics mentioned physical violence, only 12% for the decade. Only one–"Ode to Billy Joe," the plaintive ballad that spoke of suicide and love in rural Mississippi and which became the number three "single" of 1967–had violence as a predominant theme, including references to physical violence and allusions to manipulation of others. Four other lyrics, three of them primarily concerned with love, manifested violence as a secondary theme. Two of them dealt with death in auto accidents.

The only song with strong manipulation-of-others violence was "96 Tears," which concerned a boy's quest for revenge against his former sweetheart. Of all lyrics with violent assertions, "The Ballad of the Green Beret"–eulogizing valor and death in combat–achieved the highest position on the popularity charts. It was number one in 1966. No verbal violence appeared. Although more violent assertions came in the second five-year period, the increase was insignificant.

Social Protest

No Top 10 lyric in the first half of the decade made any reference to a social protest, whereas 10% of the 1965-1969 songs exhibited social protest as the predominant theme. All of these came in 1968-1969.

In contrast to statements by critics, not only did no song manifest drugs as a predominant or secondary theme, but no lyric made a clear-cut reference to drugs or to common slang terms for them. A 1969 song did mention a well-known drug advocate, but the line did not appear to be a recommendation:

> Answer for Timothy Leary, dreary
>
> [*Let the Sunshine In,* recorded by the Fifth Dimension][20]

Two other songs in that year contained phrases that might be viewed as drug-oriented–"the mind's true liberation" and "she blew my mind" –but the meanings were inconclusive in context.

SUMMARY AND CONCLUSIONS

This content analysis of lyrics of the Top 10 popular single records across the nation during each year of the sixties demonstrated that most of the songs were sung by males. Lyrics, expecially those concerned with love-sex, tended to be balanced or unhappy rather than happy. Love-sex was the predominant theme throughout the ten years.

Results tended to support the notion that more recent love songs, contrasted with those in earlier years, would evidence more domination by females, more liberal attitudes toward physical desire, and more unhappiness and balance as opposed to happiness. The tendency was only slight in some cases. The percentage of lyrics exhibiting more domination by fate than by participants increased in the second five-year period.

This differs somewhat from Carey's findings. He observed (1969a: 731) that rock-and-roll lyrics were not likely to speak of "falling in love," since that phase referred to a romantic conception of boy-girl relationships which was rejected in 1966 lyrics. Lyrics in the current analysis glorified "falling in love" through 1969. Carey asserted that the deep romantic involvement depicted in 1955 popular song lyrics often seemed to have been reduced to physical attraction in 1966 rock-and-roll lyrics. This study manifested a strong positive attitude toward romance throughout the sixties, but there were more explicit sexual assertions in lyrics of later years. Top 10 lyrics supported Carey's conclusion that rock-and-roll lyrics do not dwell on the deteriorated relationship, for, even though more songs in the first half of the decade concerned the break-up stage than any other phase, songs in the second half shifted to the prologue and happy stages.

Previous research on song lyrics has tended to center on love. This study included other variables: religion, violence, and social protest. The analysis found that few lyrics contained religious references but that negative assertions appeared in more recent years. It tended to substantiate the hypothesis that recent songs would evidence more assertions of violence, although few such references appeared. All social protests, as expected, came in later years, and the analysis disclosed no clear-cut references to drugs. Undoubtedly, allusions to drugs appeared in other songs of the sixties that did not reach the Top 10 in any year. It appears from this analysis that deviant messages in lyrics and popularity did not correlate; instead a common-denominator effect operated in songs that achieved the greatest popularity each year.

The ten number one songs in the sixties revealed no formula for popularity. One was instrumental, six were love songs, one described a dance, one extolled pride in a military group, and one expressed gratitude to a friend. Of the nine lyrics, three were happy, two unhappy, and four balanced. All were similar in that they made no reference to religion or drugs, and only one dealt with violence. In the first five years, all were love songs, three of them happy; in the second period, two of the five were love songs and four of the five were balanced. Only one top song (1967) was concerned more with physical desire than romance.

Future research might well profit by examining the annual Top 40 over a period of time and by including 33-r.p.m. albums, where many unconventional songs appear. The relative lack of attention given in communication research to recordings as a mass medium and to that medium's audiences should be remedied, for not only do popular records *entertain* listeners and *inform* them of novel and sometimes deviant messages, but they may exert a substantial *influence,* especially on the youth subculture.

NOTES

1. The authors generalized the statement from surveys of two groups of Michigan high school students responding to seven protest songs. They concluded that only 10% to 30% of their sample could write out "correct interpretations of the meanings of these songs," at least one of which ("Ode to Billy Joe") is open to varying interpretation. Another, "Lucy in the Sky With Diamonds" by the Beatles, was taken by Robinson and Hirsch to refer to LSD, but Davies (1968) asserts that the title had a more prosaic origin: the young son of Beatle John Lennon drew a picture of a schoolmate named Lucy. In the sky, she had diamonds on.

2. Carey included the national Top 30 listing from *Billboard* and the Top 30 listing from a San Francisco radio station during the same period in 1966.

3. *Billboard's* annual listings are based on relative positions and number of weeks on that publication's "Hot 100 Singles" charts, which are compiled from national retail sales and radio air time.

4. One song in the Top 10 in two different years ("The Twist" by Chubby Checker in 1960 and 1962) was counted only once. One side of a 1969 record carried two songs ("Aquarius" and "Let the Sunshine In" by the Fifth Dimension), which were analyzed separately.

5. A reliability check by five other coders on a randomly selected set of songs yielded 91% majority intercoder agreement and 70% unanimity. Intercoder agree-

ment was .747 using a more stringent measure (explained in the Note on Methodology). The unit of analysis selected was the entire song rather than the word or line because the overall message of each of the lyrics was considered the crucial factor.

6. Acuff-Rose Publications; Warner Brothers Recording Co.
7. Conrad Publishing Co.; Vee Jay Recording Co.
8. Jobete Music Co., Inc.; Motown.
9. Jobete Music Co., Inc.; Motown.
10. Acuff-Rose Publications; ABC Paramount.
11. Tyler Music Ltd.; Parrot.
12. Jobete Music Co., Inc.; Motown.
13. F.T.P. Music, Inc.; Epic.
14. Low-Twi Music, Inc.; ABC Recording Co.
15. *Blue Velvet* (1963) recorded by Bobby Vinton. Vogue Music Co.; Epic.
16. *Where Did Our Love Go* (1964) recorded by the Supremes. Jobete Music Co., Inc.; Motown.
17. Gladys Music Co.; RCA Victor.
18. Dratleaf Ltd.; Atco.
19. Publisher unknown; London.
20. United Artists Music Co., Inc.; Soul City.

REFERENCES

ADORNO, T. W. (1950) "A social critique of radio music," pp. 309-316 in B. Berelson and M. Janowitz (eds.) Public Opinion and Communication, Glencoe: Free Press.

CAREY, J. T. (1969a) "Changing courtship patterns in the popular song." Amer. J. of Sociology 74 (May): 720-731.

--- (1969b) "The ideology of autonomy in popular lyrics: a content anaylsis." Psychology 32 (May): 150-164.

DAVIES, H. (1968) The Beatles. New York: Dell.

GERSON, W. M. (1968) "Violence as an American value theme," pp. 151-162 in O. N. Larsen (ed.) Violence and the Mass Media. New York: Harper & Row.

HIRSCH, P. (1969) "The structure of the popular music industry." University of Michigan Institute for Social Research. (mimeo)

HAYAKAWA, S. I. (1957) "Popular songs vs. the facts of life," pp. 393-403 in B. Rosenberg and D. M. White (eds.) Mass Culture. Glencoe: Free Press.

HORTON, D. (1957) "The dialogue of courtship in popular songs." Amer. J. of Sociology 52 (May): 569-578.

JOHNSTONE, J. and E. KATZ (1957) "Youth and popular music: a study in the sociology of taste." Amer. J. of Sociology 62 (May): 563-568.

PEATMAN, J. G. (1944) "Radio and popular music," pp. 335-393 in P. Lazarsfeld and F. N. Stanton (eds.) Radio Research 1942-43. New York: Duell, Sloan & Pearce.

RIESMAN, D. (1957) "Listening to popular music," pp. 408-417 in B. Rosenberg and D. M. White (eds.) Mass Culture. Glencoe: Free Press.

ROBINSON, J. P. and P. J. HIRSCH (1969) "Teenage response to rock and roll protest songs." University of Michigan Institute of Social Research. (mimeo)

SCOTT, W. A. (1955) "Reliability of content analysis: the case of nominal scale coding." Public Opinion Q. 19 (Fall): 321-325.

SEBALD, H. (1968) Adolescence: A Sociological Analysis. New York: Appleton-Century-Crofts.

SMITH, E. A. (1962) American Youth Culture: Group Life in Teenage Society. New York: Free Press.

Pop Music in an English Secondary School System

ROGER L. BROWN
MICHAEL O'LEARY
University of Leicester (England)

In England, youth culture has commonly been thought of as a working-class phenomenon. For example, Abrams (1959) has argued that:

> The teenage market is almost entirely working-class. Its middle-class members are either still at school and college or else only just beginning on their careers . . . and it is highly probable, therefore, that not far short of 90 per cent of all teenage spending is conditioned by working-class taste and values. The aesthetic of the teenage market is essentially a working-class aesthetic.

Abrams, however, defined "teenagers" as unmarried people between the ages of 15 and 25.

But the English notion of a working-class youth culture has been fed from other sources as well. English educational sociology over the last two decades has emphasized relationships between social class, academic achievement, and social mobility via the educational system. An antipathy between working-class culture and middle-class values and assumptions of the secondary school has frequently been noted, and working-class adolescents have sometimes been presented not only as lacking the values and cultural interests of their middle-class counterparts but as having a distinctive set of teenage interests growing out of their marginal status in the educational system.

Sugarman (1967) notes that one traditional view of the matter is that of young people who are:

> exposed to the temptations of a youth culture that encourages, at the least, a considerable diversion of time and energy from educational pursuits and, at most, an inversion of the related values of deferred gratification, academic achievement and conformity to rules.

Sugarman's own findings from a study of London schoolboys lend support to this hypothesis. Involvement in youth culture, as indexed by frequency of smoking, dating, and listening to pop music radio stations, was shown to be inversely related to comitment to the norms of the school and such middle-class values as deferred gratification.

But Sugarman, in discussing his results, makes an important distinction between youth culture and the teenage social system. He points out that a youth culture, while it may be opposed in its values to the school or middle-class society, may yet be dependent for its existence on the patterns of association brought into being and maintained by the school. Sugarman refers to the research by Coleman (1961) in Illinois schools in pointing out that the dominant form of youth culture in America is institutionally based in the high school. Coleman, of course, argues that, despite this, the values of the American youth culture are antipathetic to academic values.

In the analysis of various types of youth culture and their relationship to the educational system there are thus two related questions that may be posed. In the first place, is adherence to a particular form of youth culture generated outside the school or inside it? And second, what is the relationship of any youth culture to the values of the school?

The development of pop music in Britain over the last fifteen years has commonly been taken as evidence for the emergence of a distinctive youth culture. Indeed, those who view contemporary youth culture as one form of commercial mass culture have tended to argue that the evolution of a distinctive set of adolescent tastes has been the result of the growth of industries, including a section of the music industry, which have set themselves the task of building a distinctive adolescent market. It, therefore, seemed worthwhile to investigate whether the adolescent following for pop music conformed to any of the youth culture paradigms already discussed.

THE RESEARCH SETTING AND METHODS USED

The survey reported here was conducted in three secondary schools in Leicestershire, England. Two high schools feed the third, an upper school.

Under the Leicestershire Plan, all pupils transfer to a high school at the age of 11+ and remain there for at least the first three years of secondary schooling. At the end of the third year, pupils may decide to remain in the high school for another year–until they reach the minimum legal leaving age of 15; or, they may decide to transfer to the upper school for an additional period of at least two years. In the schools studied, nearly two-thirds of all pupils transferred to the upper school.

The sample included all those in the third, fourth, and fifth years of secondary education. More specifically, this meant the entire third year in each of the high schools, the entire fourth year in the upper school (those who had transferred for this and at least one further year), plus the "rump" group in each high school–comprising those who were intending to leave school as soon as possible. The entire fifth year in the upper school was also included.

Respondents completed two self-administered questionnaires–the first dealing with pop music and communication behaviors and the second with friendship patterns, attitudes toward school, and demographic variables.

Integration into the teenage culture was assessed in a variety of ways. Respondents were asked to name song hits currently in the Top 10 as a measure of knowledge. They also were asked to compare their own knowledge with that of friends and to rate how interested they were in this type of music. Youngsters also provided data on radio listening, record buying, and talking with friends about pop music. Respondents were asked to name other adolescents who were their friends and also those who were regarded as particularly prestigeful in a number of specified ways. The vast majority of these sociometric nominations fell within the bounds of the sample.

The position of each adolescent within the social class and school structure was also determined. Father's occupation provided the index of social class. The two groups used in the present analysis–middle and working–divide roughly at a point between lower white-collar employees and skilled manual workers.

Students' prospects within the educational system furnished the second major independent variable. Rather than relying on intelligence scores or other objective data, teachers' assessments of each pupil's academic performance were used. The teacher (or in some cases the headteacher) of each class member judged his likelihood of academic achievement according to the most difficult public examination he was likely to pass.

This measure of educational prospects has certain advantages in light of American studies that show the self-fulfilling effects of teachers' expectations regarding students (Rosenthal and Jacobson, 1968). When we examine adolescents' absorption into the teen culture in terms of low, medium, and high "achievement," we are distinguishing children according to a socially visible set of abilities, personality, and interests that affect their treatment in a school system largely guided by middle-class values.

FRIENDSHIP, PRESTIGE, AND ADOLESCENTS' ENTERTAINMENT

Before examining the joint relationships of social class and school attainment with exposure to the teen culture, we should take note of how adolescents' use of entertainment is integrated into the peer social system.

It is clear from the survey data that interest and involvement in pop music were related to the social systems found in the three schools. Both knowledge of and interest in the Top 10 were related to the number of times a boy or girl was nominated as a friend. In general, the more friendship nominations received, the higher the level of knowledge. In terms of interest, it was only those who received *no* nominations who expressed a markedly lower level of interest that the rest of the sample.

These data, of course, do not provide evidence about the nature of the relationships between involvement with pop music and integration into a pattern of friendships. It obviously is possible for a certain level of knowledge to be required for admittance into a particular clique as well as for clique membership to be a means of gaining knowledge and stimulating interest.

Adolescents in the sample, besides being asked to name their friends, also were requested to record the names of those they regarded as knowledgeable about pop music, those they regarded as popular, and those they regarded as leaders. Each respondent was scored for the number of expertness, popularity, and leadership ratings he received.

Correlations were computed between these three measures of social integration and actual knowledge of the Top 10—separately for boys and girls. As one might expect, the three dimensions of sociometric choice intercorrelate highly. A reputation for knowledge about hit tunes is strongly associated with nominations for popularity and leadership.

To some extent, this reputation is justified by adolescents' actual knowledge of what is currently popular. Gamma correlations between knowledge and reputation as an expert are .38 for boys and .30 for girls.

A more comprehensive picture of the relationships between social integration and knowledge about hits emerges when a number of analytic controls are made. Let us assume that general popularity among one's peers is antecedent to being regarded as a music expert. Popularity confers a social visibility that can reveal details of one's integration into the entertainment culture. Actual knowledge of current hits is treated as another antecedent to reputation as an expert; it is the "reality base" on which peers' judgments are made.

Table 1 shows how reputation as an expert varies as a function of general popularity and actual knowledge. Boys and girls have been merged because patterns in their data are similar.

Reputation as an expert increases with each antecedent–popularity (thought of as conferring visibility) and actual knowledge. Even among unpopular respondents–those receiving no peer nominations–reputation is associated with knowledge. This testifies to the central importance of hit tunes and to adolescents' awareness of how others in the peer culture orient toward music. Children at the periphery of their peer group nonetheless, can establish a reputation for knowledge about this type of entertainment.

The joint effect of who-you-know and what-you-know is revealed by noting that among the unknowledgeable and upopular 23% have a music reputation, compared to 89% for the knowledgeable and highly popular.

Further insight into the importance of knowledge about pop music in the acquisition of social prestige is provided in Table 2. A series of questions asked sample members to say how frequently they compared themselves with peers along a number of dimensions. One of these was

TABLE 1
REPUTATION AS A POP MUSIC EXPERT, BY GENERAL POPULARITY AND KNOWLEDGE OF HIT TUNES

Knowledge of Hit Tunes		Low	Medium	High
		Obtaining 1+ nominations as pop music expert		
Nominations as popular	0	23% (n = 121)	50% (n = 119)	55% (n = 57)
	1-2	48% (n = 90)	57% (n = 90)	68% (n = 46)
	3+	69% (n = 52)	85% (n = 65)	89% (n = 38)

TABLE 2
SOCIAL COMPARISON OF POP MUSIC KNOWLEDGE BY GENERAL POPULARITY AND REPUTATION AS A MUSIC EXPERT

Nominations as Pop Music Expert		0	1-2	3+
		Comparing own pop music knowledge frequently with that of peers		
Nominations as popular	0	44% (n = 181)	66% (n = 80)	89% (n = 35)
	1	47% (n = 99)	56% (n = 81)	70% (n = 43)
	2+	50% (n = 30)	54% (n = 48)	63% (n = 67)

musical knowledge. Table 2 shows that adolescents with a reputation for knowledge reported more comparison activities than those without a reputation–irrespective of how popular they were. Popularity, on the other hand, is not consistently associated with comparison behavior. There is a tendency for popularity and comparison to go together among the inexpert children, but the reverse is true among children who have a music reputation.

These findings suggest a dual explanation of comparison behavior in the pop music field. Among the inexpert, the situation appears simple: greater popularity indicates a higher level of peer activity and hence more opportunities for comparison. Among the expert and unpopular, however, the particularly high level of comparison behavior may indicate some anxiety that music knowledge has not led to a consequent and expected degree of popularity. Comparison behavior here may index more than simple involvement.

A final point about social comparisons concerns sex differences. Of the several variables that predict interest and involvement in pop music, sex is the most evident, with girls regularly scoring higher on most indices. There is an apparent anomaly, though. While girls could correctly name more of the Top 10 than boys, girls, more than boys, were apt to think of themselves as like other persons in knowledge of music.

It may be that adolescents tend to compare their musical knowledge with peers of the same sex. Greater interest among girls, which is generally recognized by these adolescents, might limit variability in the girls' social comparisons.

SOCIAL CLASS, PROSPECTS IN SCHOOL, AND ABSORPTION INTO TEEN CULTURE

Results discussed thus far disclose the centrality of popular music in the teenage social system. We turn now to an analysis of how adolescents' exposure to teen culture relates to structural factors–social class and success at school. Table 3 reports data on exposure to pop music according to class and rated prospects in school.

In general, it appears that differences due to academic achievement are greater than those due to social class. Well over half of all respondents had a radio of their own, but high achievers in both middle and working classes are less likely to have one than those at the two lower achievement levels.

The self-completion questionnaires contained questions about frequency of listening to both Radio 1, the national BBC network that mainly broadcasts pop and light music, and to Radio Luxembourg, which has a similar output. In general, as Table 3 shows, frequency of radio listening increases with decreasing academic achievement, while social class, in most cases, makes little difference. However, among those at the lowest

TABLE 3
POP MUSIC EXPOSURE, BY SOCIAL CLASS AND SCHOOL ACHIEVEMENT (in percentages)

Social Class	Middle			Working		
Achievement	Low	Medium	High	Low	Medium	High
Having radio of own						
	69	69	58	61	68	55
Listening to Radio I on weekdays for 1+ hours						
	62	59	55	74	58	58
Listening to Radio Luxembourg on weekdays for 1+ hours						
	50	42	38	50	44	45
Watching "Top of the Pops" on BBC 1 most weeks						
	76	75	73	77	84	67
Having a record player						
	89	91	81	79	84	79
Buying 2+ "singles" in last six weeks						
	40	34	28	40	40	30
Buying an LP in last three months						
	33	30	21	23	24	24
n =	67	58	146	167	57	92

achievement level, middle-class respondents listen less frequently to Radio 1 than working-class respondents, while working-class high achievers listen to Radio Luxembourg somewhat more frequently than their middle-class counterparts.

Viewing "Top of the Pops," the well-established, early evening pop music program on the BBC's main television channel, does not vary consistently with either social class or academic achievement, although working-class high achievers watch somewhat less often, and working-class medium achievers somewhat more often, than their middle-class counterparts.

Well over three-quarters of all the adolescents in the sample claimed to have a record player of their own. Working-class respondents at the lower achievement levels are somewhat less likely than their middle-class counterparts to have such equipment. (A simple economic explanation is obviously possible here.)

As with some of the other indices of pop music exposure already discussed, record purchasing also varies with achievement level, though not with social class. The purchase of "singles" is more frequent at the lower achievement levels in both class groups, though the same relationship holds for LPs only in the middle class.

The data in Table 3, despite a number of anomalies, certainly suggest that those at the highest level of achievement are less exposed to pop music than those at the lower levels but that class differences are relatively unimportant.

Differences between the same six groups on involvement in pop music may be examined in Table 4. It is apparent that levels of knowledge do not differ in a uniform way between groups. Working-class medium-level achievers are more likely than other groups to be able to name five or more of the current Top 10. This anomaly may result from a finding shown on the bottom line of the table: the same group was more likely than the other five groups to talk frequently with peers about pop music.

More important, the generally inverse relationship between exposure to pop music and academic achievement noted in Table 3 manifests itself again in Table 4. A smaller proportion of those at the highest achievement level in each social-class category wanted to know a lot more about pop music when compared to those at the two lower levels of achievement. In terms of the groups more likely to receive nominations from peers as comprising individuals particularly knowledgeable about pop music, the dividing line falls between the medium- and low-achievement levels, with the low achievers in both social classes being more likely than other groups to receive at least one nomination as a pop music expert.

TABLE 4
INVOLVEMENT IN POP MUSIC, BY SOCIAL CLASS AND SCHOOL ACHIEVEMENT (in percentages)

Social Class	Middle			Working		
Achievement	Low	Medium	High	Low	Medium	High
Correctly naming 5+ of the Top 10	39	38	42	37	53	44
Interested in knowing current Top 10	86	71	71	72	79	74
Frequently wishing to know more about pop music	62	62	33	63	64	35
Receiving 1+ nominations as pop music expert	60	46	50	64	50	46
Frequently talking to friends about pop music	62	68	62	62	78	65
n =	67	58	146	167	57	92

As we have already seen, the importance of pop music to respondents was investigated by asking them to state how often they compared their own knowledge with that of their peers. It was felt that frequent comparisons indicate pop music is considered an important source of social prestige. At the same time as they provided this information, sample members also said how often they compared themselves with peers along a number of other dimensions thought likely to be important to them. Table 5 sets out the resulting data for the six groups derived from the cross-tabulation of social class and academic achievement.

In general, the figures indicate that comparing oneself with peers in terms of school performance becomes more common with increasing academic achievement, while the reverse is true for all other areas where comparing tends to be most common in low-achievement groups.

In the case of comparisons with peers in terms of knowledge of pop music, percentages are generally lower than those for school performance and out-of-school clothes but higher than those for television. Looking across the table, music comparisons increase as one moves from the high- to the medium-achievement group in both class categories, but there are no differences between the classes. In the middle class the percentage rises further as one moves to the low-achievement group, but in the working class the figure falls, so that middle-class low achievers are likely to compare themselves along this dimension more frequently than are working-class low achievers.

TABLE 5
COMPARING BEHAVIOR, BY SOCIAL CLASS AND SCHOOL ACHIEVEMENT (in percentages)

Social Class	Middle			Working		
Achievement	Low	Medium	High	Low	Medium	High
Comparing frequently: School performance	73	69	80	50	63	75
Knowledge of pop music	63	58	46	54	58	45
Knowledge of TV programs	52	33	24	46	41	29
Kind of house lived in	51	48	22	44	30	29
Out-of-school clothes	74	69	70	72	68	69
Number of friends	50	33	28	48	31	29
Social skills	68	63	44	61	50	49
n =	67	58	146	167	57	92

A rather similar picture is seen in the case of comparisons with peers about knowledge of television programs. At the two higher achievement levels, a somewhat higher proportion of working-class as against middle-class respondents claimed to compare their own knowledge frequently, but among low achievers more middle-class than working-class respondents made this claim.

However, the important message in Table 5 is found in the overall pattern of data. Apart from the special case of school performance itself, lower academic achievement led to a greater likelihood of frequent comparisons with peers along a number of dimensions. The general pattern for pop music and television programs not only parallels that for comparisons in terms of number of friends and social skills but also for the kind of house in which the respondent lived, where, on the basis of the likely objective situation, one might have expected some clearer social-class differences.

The table leads to the argument that pop music is not only an area in which these adolescents frequently compare themselves with peers, but is also is part of a general set of social comparison topics–not all of which reflect peer social activity–where frequency of comparison is associated with adolescents' prospects for educational advancement. Considering the lifetime status implications of failure at school in the British system, these frequent comparisons with peers may perhaps reflect a generalized anxiety growing out of a realization that one's chances of passing public examinations are relatively slim.

Put another way, the findings reported in Tables 3, 4, and 5 suggest that involvement in the teen culture is more a function of where youngsters are headed in the social structure than where they have come from in terms of parental status. Characterizing the teen culture as lower class in origin may be less accurate than describing it as lower class in destination. (We return to this argument below.) Firmer conclusions about this could be drawn if the survey had included measures of occupational and life-style aspirations.

Support for the contention that the institutional base for interest in pop music lay in the schools rather than in the outside social structure also is provided by data of a different sort. We already have seen that interest in pop music is related to the total number of friendship nominations a boy or girl received. Respondents in the survey also were asked to name separately those they were friendly with "at school" and those they were friendly with "out of school." It thus was possible to classify sample members simultaneously in terms of the number of nominations they received in each of these spheres.

Analysis shows that the percentage correctly naming one or more of the Top 10 increases with the number of at-school friendship nominations but does not increase with the number of out-of-school nominations. Indeed, among those who received fewer than two at-school nominations, knowledge about pop music decreases with the number of out-of-school nominations. Knowledge–and interest in knowing the Top 10–were especially low among the minority of youngsters who received more mentions as out-of-school friends than in-school friends.

These findings lend added support to the idea that interest and involvement in pop music form part of the usual pattern of interests of the adolescent social system located within school and are largely dependent on school as an institutional base. Those whose social life lies outside the school orbit, rather than within it (as indexed by friendship nominations), tend to be less knowledgeable about and less interested in pop music than others.

DISCUSSION

The data from these three schools certainly do not suggest the existence of a class-based youth culture explicable simply in terms of the larger social system. Social-class differences in pop music exposure and involvement were not large (and indeed the fact that such exposure and involvement were widespread should not be forgotten).

We have argued that the schools provided the institutional base for the development of a pop music following. However, this may have been partly a simple reflection of the fact that there was a relative lack of other meeting places for youth in the small town and village where the study was conducted. But it seems that the school system's role can be described more exactly than this. The school carries out a continuous assessment of pupils' progress in terms of a dominant value–academic performance. As the data indicate, those seen as high academic achievers were, in general, less involved in pop music than low achievers. We, therefore, can argue that academic work and pop music were, to some extent at least, alternative foci of interest–and even alternative sources of reputation. Those who failed to shine academically may have turned alternatively to pop music as a source of peer group prestige.

There are some indications that middle-class low achievers were particularly involved in pop music. Table 4 indicates that this group was particularly interested in knowing the Top 10, and Table 5 shows that this group also scored particularly high in terms of pop music comparing behavior. Given normative expectations on the part of school and parents that middle-class offspring should "do well" academically, subsequent failure in terms of teacher assessments may lead to an anxious search for alternative kinds of achievement. To some extent, there may be a withdrawal from the demands of the larger system and a pursuit of the easier goal of a pop music reputation within the peer group. Table 5 shows that the middle-class low achievers were the group most likely to compare themselves in terms of social skills. Ability in this area may again be more important for those whose school performance falls below expectations. The openness of the Leicestershire Plan system–where any youngster has the right to move on from high to upper school–may serve to accentuate the consequences of a discrepancy between class origin and academic performance. Table 5 shows that comparisons about school performance increased at the higher achievement levels among the working-class adolescents but that middle-class low achievers also scored high. This too may indicate anxiety on the part of the latter group.

Further research should clearly seek to establish the relationships between the peer group system and the results of interaction between social class and academic performance. Low achievers, and particularly those from middle-class origins, may be drawn progressively towards peer groups where pop music knowledgeability is a valued commodity and where academic rating is of only minor importance. Even so, our data do not suggest that this process is accompanied by the development of any antipathy toward the school. On the contrary, those with less positive attitudes toward school were found to be less knowledgeable. It also would be worth examining the relationships between low academic achievement, a low degree of peer group integration, low pop music involvement, and the decision to leave school at the minimum age. Prestige based on a pop music reputation, although alternative to academic prestige, may be an integrating agent making continuance in school a more acceptable course of action. This process may be more likely in situations like the present, where a developed adolescent social system outside the school was largely absent.

REFERENCES

ABRAMS, M. (1959) The Teenage Consumer. London: London Press Exchange.
COLEMAN, J. S. (1961) The Adolescent Society. New York: Free Press.
ROSENTHAL, R., and L. JACOBSON (1968) Pygmalion in the Classroom. New York: Holt, Rinehart & Winston.
SUGARMAN, B. (1967) "Involvement in youth culture, academic achievement and conformity in school, an empirical study of London schoolboys." British J. of Sociology 18 (June): 151-164.

Family and Media Influences On Adolescent Consumer Learning

SCOTT WARD
Harvard University

DANIEL WACKMAN
University of Minnesota

The focus of this paper is on "consumer learning" processes–i.e., processes by which adolescents acquire skills and attitudes relating to the consumption of goods and services. We examine intrafamily and mass media communication as they affect consumer learning processes, and describe some demographic predictors of consumer learning.

While the area of consumer learning has received little attention in published research sources (Herrmann, 1969), it would seem to be an important area for research for several reasons. Young people comprise a large specialized market segment for many products and services. They influence purchases within family and peer groups. In addition, childhood and adolescent experiences relating to consumption presumably affect patterns of consumer behavior in adult life.

From the point of view of communication research, the area of consumer learning is important for two reasons. First, television adver-

---

Authors' Note: *This research was supported by the National Institute of Mental Health "Social Effects of Television" research program (contract HSM 42-70-74) and by a grant from the Marketing Science Institute, Cambridge, Mass. The authors wish to acknowledge the help of Greg Reale, Northwestern University and MSI, for research assistance, and Wing Hing Tsang, MSI, for computer assistance.*

tising comprises a large amount of air time. On the average, between one and two of every ten minutes is devoted to advertising. Commercials are the number three content category, behind movies (32%) and comedy-variety (17%) but ahead of action (13%) and eight other categories (Steiner, 1963). Therefore, young people are likely to be exposed to a great deal of television advertising. In light of the high incidence of television advertising, it is particularly surprising that communication research has focused on effects of television programming on young people, to the virtual exclusion of examination of effects of television advertising.

A second reason for the relevance of consumer learning to communication research is that the area offers the possibility of studying effects of communication on overt behavior, as reported by adolescents.

BACKGROUND

Research relevant for the study of adolescent consumer learning is typically of two types: research examining family consumer processes, and research examining consumption-related variables within static age groups of children. Research examining family processes, however, usually is limited to consideration of husband-wife dyads (Granbois, 1967; Kenkel, 1961; Komarovsky, 1961; Pollay, 1969; Wolgast, 1958). Little systematic evidence exists concerning the role of parent-child interaction in affecting consumer learning processes of offspring (see Ward and Robertson, 1970).

Research focusing on static age groups has examined such topics as attitudes toward saving versus spending and marginal propensities to consume (Cateora, 1963; Phelan and Schvaneveldt, 1969). Additionally, research has examined developing patterns of consumer behavior among young children to commercial messages (Wells, 1965, 1966).

Communication research, on the other hand, has generally ignored television advertising's effects on young people, while concentrating on programming effects. Published studies of advertising's effects have generally focused on adults rather than on young people (Steiner, 1963; Bauer and Greyser, 1968).

Nevertheless several points of view developed in consumer and communication research are relevant to the present study of family and media communication influences on consumer learning. With respect to the independent and mediating variables in the present research, communication research has examined the interaction of family and mass media as primary factors in socialization processes, especially political socialization (see Chaffee et al., 1967; Jennings and Niemi, 1968; Hess and Torney, 1967). Communication research has also focused on reasons for watching television (Greenberg and Dominick, 1968), in addition to simple measures of time spent watching, which characterized earlier media research.

With respect to the dependent variables, recent research has demonstrated that communication effects—particularly mass communication effects—do not operate in simple stimulus-response fashion (Klapper, 1960; Bauer, 1963). It would also be inaccurate, however, to consider communication as merely a reinforcer of existing cognitive states or behavioral patterns, as one prevalent view of mass media effects would have it (Klapper, 1960). Most of the evidence for this point of view is from studies of attitude change. However, socialization processes are characterized by attitude formation and learning processes. Thus, variables other than attitude change, such as attitude formation and learning, more accurately indicate mass communication effects, and, perhaps, predict behavioral effects.

In the present research, our interest is in four criterion variables: recall of commercial content, attitudes toward television advertising, materialistic attitudes, and self-reported effects of commercials on buying behavior. We expect that various demographic indices will be related to these criterion variables. Our interest is in demographic characteristics of adolescents which, in effect, "locate" the adolescent in the social environment, such as socioeconomic status, intelligence, and available money.

Within demographically defined groups, however, we expect that adolescent consumer learning will vary depending on the relative presence or absence of intrafamily communication about consumption matters, and the adolescent's media use. Our concern is with two dimensions of media use: amount of print and television use, and motivations or reasons adolescents watch television commercials. Thus we are concerned with the *reasons* adolescents watch commercials, as well as with the amount of television and print use.

Previous writers suggest that people may attend to mass media communication for social reasons. For example, by watching commercials they may form impressions of what kinds of people buy certain products or brands, and they may develop associations of products with various life styles (Ogilvy, 1963). These "social utility" reasons for watching commercials may provide a means of conforming to the perceived expectations of others—that is, individuals may feel that if they buy a certain product or brand, they can manipulate the impression others have of them (Ward and Gibson, 1969).

Individuals may also attend to mass communication in order to provide a basis for later interpersonal communication (Chaffee and McLeod, 1967). Such "communication utility" motivations may also apply to watching television commercials.

Finally, people may attend to commercials as a means of vicarious participation in desired life styles, or as a means of vicarious association with attractive others.

To summarize our focus in this research, we are interested in the development of consumer learning among adolescents. Previous work in consumer behavior and research in communication and socialization processes suggest that family communication processes and media variables should relate to our criterion variables. However, we expect that demographic variables, which serve as social locators for adolescents, will affect these processes. Additionally, we expect that the criterion variables will be related to the motivations or reasons adolescents attend to commercials–for reasons of "social utility" (i.e., gauging what others will think if certain buying behaviors occur), "Communication utility" (attending to commercials in order to provide a basis for later interpersonal communication), and "vicarious consumption" (watching commercials as a means of identifying with desired life styles).

METHODS

Data for this study are from a 1970 survey of 1,094 eighth through twelfth graders in the Prince Georges County, Maryland, school district. The adolescents received self-administered questionnaries in randomly selected classrooms in twelve schools. The questionnaries took about 45 minutes (one class period) to complete.

While Prince Georges County provides a good cross-section of American social classes, the sample distribution slightly overrepresents the middle class. This may result from the undersampling of classrooms from predominantly Black schools. Due to racial tensions at the time of the survey, these schools refused to permit questionnaire distribution.

The sample is divided into junior high school students (eighth and ninth grades n=537) and senior high school students (tenth, eleventh, and twelfth grades, n=557).

The variables in this research consist of scales formed by summing several items.[1] The procedure for developing the scales was to factor-analyze items relevant to areas of a priori interest where appropriate. Items which failed to load on the hypothesized factors were discarded and remaining items were summed to form the scale.

RESULTS

A primary concern is the extent to which different kinds of consumer learning change over time; or, to put it somewhat differently, what developmental changes occur during adolescence in different kinds of consumer learning. Comparisons between junior and senior high respondents indicate no differences on the several learning criteria—recall, attitudes, materialism, and effects on buying behavior. Thus it would appear that there are no gross developmental changes during the adolescent period, at least in terms of our criteria of four kinds of consumer learning shown in Table 1.

In contrast to the lack of differences on the criterion variables, however, we find differences between junior and senior high respondents on nearly every communication variable. In general, younger adolescents engage in more communication and are more likely to watch commercials for social utility reasons than older adolescents. The data in Table 1 also indicate that younger adolescents watch more television than older adolescents and talk more with their parents about consumption. Younger

TABLE 1
CONSUMER LEARNING AND COMMUNICATION VARIABLES BY AGE GROUP[a]

	Younger	Older	Differences
Recall of ads	12.4	12.3	n.s.
Attitudes toward TV ads	6.2	6.1	n.s.
Materialism	13.4	13.4	n.s.
Effects of ads on buying	0.7	0.7	n.s.
Exposure to TV	3.6	2.8	Y > O
Exposure to magazines	2.6	2.6	n.s.
Family communication about consumption	8.8	7.5	Y > O
Social utility reasons	6.0	4.7	Y > O
Communication utility reasons	1.6	1.1	Y > O
Vicarious consumption reasons	2.6	2.4	n.s.

a. Table entries are the mean scores for the age group on particular scales. Unless n.s. indicated, differences between younger and older samples are significant at the .05 level or beyond.

and older adolescents are equal in their use of magazines. Furthermore, while junior high respondents watch television commercials for social and communicatory utility reasons to a greater extent than senior high respondents, the two groups do not differ in watching TV commercials for vicarious consumption reasons.

These results suggest that although younger and older adolescents may be at the same level in terms of consumer learning, the processes of learning may differ for the two age groups. Mean scores for the two groups differ on the independent and mediating variables. We defer a closer examination of this question until later.

A second consideration is to examine to what extent the different kinds of consumer learning occur together or occur independently of each other. Moreover, do the patterns of relationships among the criterion variables change over time? If the relationships among the criterion variables were stronger for older than for younger adolescents, this would indicate an increase in the integration of different aspects of consumer learning during adolescence. However, this kind of development does not seem to occur, as can be seen in Table 2. Correlations among the criterion variables for both younger and older adolescents are nearly all essentially zero. Thus, it would seem that the several criteria of consumer learning we have used in this study are quite independent of each other, including the general orientation measures of attitudes toward advertising and materialism.

DIFFERENCES IN CONSUMER LEARNING BETWEEN YOUNGER AND OLDER ADOLESCENTS

The remainder of the analysis concerns differences in consumer learning processes for younger and older adolescents. Our procedure is to examine

TABLE 2

CORRELATIONS AMONG CONSUMER LEARNING VARIABLES FOR YOUNGER AND OLDER ADOLESCENTS[a]

	Recall	Attitudes	Materialism	Effects on Buying
Recall of ads	–	-.01	-.08	.08
Attitudes toward TV ads	.08	–	.05	.04
Materialism	.01	.07	–	.11
Effects of ads on buying	.05	.13	.06	–

a. Table entries are product-moment correlation coefficients. Entries in the upper right triangle of the matrix are correlations for younger adolescents; entries in the lower left triangle are correlations for older adolescents.

the relationship between a set of independent variables and each criterion variable.

With each criterion variable, a step-up regression analysis was conducted with three sets of independent variables. Demographic variables included the adolescent's social class, available money, and intelligence. Communication variables included amount of time spent watching television yesterday, number of magazines subscribed to and read, and amount of family communication about consumption. Reasons for watching television commercials included social utility, communicatory utility, and vicarious consumption reasons. Analyses were carried out separately for younger and older adolescents.

Recall of Television Advertising

Recall of television advertising is a measure of the simplest kind of consumer learning, basically indicating an awareness of the themes and slogans of American companies and consumer products. For younger adolescents, the respondents' intelligence and their magazine reading were the two variables that met our criterion of accounting for at least one percent of the variance of the criterion variable. As can be seen in Table 3, intelligence was a much better predictor of recall than exposure to magazines. For older adolescents, intelligence was again the strongest predictor, with television time as the only other important predictor.

Intelligence, which in school tests mainly reflects verbal skills, is the primary predictor of commercial retention. Perhaps one should not be surprised that amount of media exposure is a less certain correlate. Considering the redundancy of commerical messages, it takes limited contact with the media to gain exposure to most prominant ads. However, storing and retrieving their content depend on the verbal skills that govern performance at a wide range of communicatory tasks in modern society.

Attitudes Toward Television Advertising

Attitudes toward television advertising are a measure of a more complex kind of consumer learning. Table 3 indicates that, among younger adolescents, two variables accounted for much of the variance: social utility reasons for viewing commercials, and time spent watching television. By contrast, among older adolescents three different variables accounted for much of the variance: vicarious consumption reasons for viewing commercials, family communication about consumption, and

TABLE 3
RELATIONSHIPS BETWEEN RECALL OF ADS, ATTITUDES TOWARD TV ADVERTISING, MATERIALISM, EFFECTS OF ADVERTISING ON BUYING, AND THE INDEPENDENT VARIABLES FOR YOUNGER AND OLDER ADOLESCENTS[a]

	Recall		Attitudes		Materialism		Effects	
	Young	Old	Young	Old	Young	Old	Young	Old
Socioeconomic status	.07	.08	.02	**-.11**	.06	-.02	-.01	.02
Intelligence	**.34**[b]	**.29**	.04	.07	.07	**-.17**	.06	.02
Available money	.00	.01	.07	.08	**.11**	.01	.07	.08
Family communication	.00	.06	.06	**.13**	.03	.07	**.18**	**.26**
TV exposure	.10	**.16**	**.10**	.03	-.01	-.07	-.09	-.09
Print exposure	**.13**	.07	.01	.04	.07	-.01	.12	-.03
Social utility	.06	.06	**.14**	.02	**.17**	**.11**	**.21**	**.08**
Communication utility	.01	.02	.03	.06	.09	.05	**-.16**	**.08**
Vicarious consumption	-.02	.02	.06	**.16**	**.11**	**.17**	**.12**	-.03
Multiple correlation coefficient (R)	.39	.31	.25	.29	.34	.38	.37	.31

a. Cell entries are beta-weights between the independent variables and the four dependent variables. These standardized partial regression coefficients represent the relationship between the independent and the dependent variable with all other independent variables controlled.

b. The boldface entries indicate those variables, when added in the step-up regression equation, increased the amount of variance accounted for by at least one percent.

socioeconomic status. Thus, it would appear that markedly different processes are involved for the two groups of adolescents in learning general attitudes toward advertising.

Materialism

Like attitudes toward advertising, materialism is a measure of more complex kinds of consumer learning, indicating an orientation which views material goods and money as important for personal happiness and social progress. For younger adolescents, three factors accounted for much of the variance: social utility, vicarious consumption reasons for viewing

TV commercials, and the amount of money an adolescent usually has available. Similarly, for older adolescents, social utility and vicarious consumption reasons for viewing commercials were also important predictor variables; however, the third variable for this age group was intelligence, which was negatively related to materialism.

These results suggest that among both age groups, the processes involved in learning a materialistic orientation are quite similar and quite strongly related to the adolescent's television viewing behavior, especially reasons for watching commercials.

EFFECTS OF TELEVISION ADVERTISING ON BUYING BEHAVIOR

Our measure of effects of television advertising on buying behavior is a self-report item which asks whether the adolescent feels he has been directly influenced by television advertising in buying a specific product. This variable is essentially a measure of behavioral effects of advertising.

Table 3 indicates that three variables are important predictors of this kind of learning for both younger and older adolescents: communication in the family about consumption, social utility reasons for viewing television commercials, and the amount of exposure to magazines. In addition, for younger adolescents, a fourth variable is important, i.e., communicatory utility reasons for viewing commercials, which is negatively related to effects of advertisements on buying.

CONSUMPTION AS A SOCIAL PROCESS

These results suggest that simple exposure to advertising is not a sufficient condition for buying behavior. Rather, other variables involving the processing of information about consumption intervene between exposure to the commercial and purchase. Communication about consumption with parents seems to be a particularly important variable intervening between exposure to commercials and actual purchase, especially among older adolescents. This finding indicates clearly that consumption behavior is a *social* process, involving overt communication with others, not simply an individual psychological process triggered by exposure to advertising.

For younger adolescents, reasons for watching commercials are also important intervening variables between exposure and purchase. Social utility reasons for viewing are positively related to purchase behavior, further supporting the interpretation that consumption behavior is a social process.

The nature of this social process requires further study, however. Communicatory utility reasons for viewing commercials correlate negatively with purchasing behavior among younger children. Thus, purchasing seems a function of social comparison motivations, but not of interest in social communication. Among older respondents, both reasons for watching commercials emerge as modest but significant correlates.

SUMMARY AND DISCUSSION

We can conclude the following from the data presented in this study:

(1) Different aspects of consumer learning are not well integrated among either younger or older adolescents.

(2) Different clusters of variables have effects on the different kinds of consumer learning examined in this study.

(3) For any particular kind of consumer learning, essentially the same cluster of variables affects that kind of learning for both younger and older adolescents. Therefore, even though younger adolescents are exposed to more commercial content on the media, talk with parents more about consumer goods, and watch commercials more for social utility and communicatory utility reasons, the predictive power of these variables is essentially the same in both groups of adolescents.

(4) Amount of exposure to television is not a very important variable in predicting different kinds of consumer learning. This finding adds to the growing body of literature which indicates that media exposure time is simply not a powerful explanatory variable of communication effects.

(5) *Three* major processes seem to be involved in the different kinds of consumer learning.

The learning of advertising slogans seems to be mainly a function of the intelligence of the adolescent.

The learning of more cognitive orientations, such as attitudes toward television advertising and a materialism orientation, seems to be mainly a function of the adolescent's reasons for viewing commercials. Thus, these cognitive orientations develop as a function of the adolescent's television behavior, but not simply of his exposure time. Rather, the orientations develop as a function of the uses the adolescent makes of commercial content, several of which are basically social uses.

A third process, which seems to be involved in the learning of purchasing behaviors, is clearly an *overt social process*. In this process, communication with parents about advertising, consumer goods, and consumption processes seems to be an important variable intervening between exposure to advertising and the purchase of consumer goods.

This finding, indicating the occurrence of an overt social process between exposure to the media and decision-making, is similar to Chaffee and McLeod's (1967) finding regarding the occurrence of an overt social process between exposure to political content on the media and voting decision. Further, our finding that adolescents use commercials for social purposes parallels their finding that media political content is used for social purposes as well as for making political decisions.

Adolescents' consumer learning is not simply an individual stimulus-response phenomenon, but is a social learning process. It may be fruitful to think of media advertising as shaping the content and form of interpersonal perceptions and communication, rather than considering the media as dispensers of product information. Cross-sectional research with wider age samples than studied here would help reveal developmental changes in youngsters' consumer orientations.

NOTES

1. The following is a summary of the indices used in the present study:

INDEX	OPERATIONAL DEFINITION	MEASURE
Socioeconomic status: social class	Duncan socioeconomic index	5-digit occupational code, including 3-digit IRS code, 2-digit code indicating population decile of occupation
Intelligence	School test scores (IQ, and the like)	Track in school
Available money	Total money acquired in average week	Open-end item concerning allowance, jobs, "all other ways" money acquired
Family communication about consumption	Overt parent-adolescent interactions concerning consumption of goods and services	4-point "often-never" items, such as: "How often do you ask your parents for advice about buying things?"
Quantity of media use:		
A. television	Self-reported average time spent watching television, time spent watching yesterday	Open-end responses to questions about time spent with TV yesterday
B. print	Self-reported subscriptions and readership of magazines	Open-end items for periodical subscriptions or readership

INDEX	OPERATIONAL DEFINITION	MEASURE
Reasons for watching commercials:		
A. social utility	Motivation to watch commercials as a means of gathering information about life styles and behaviors associated with uses of specific consumer products	4-point agree-disagree items. Scales such as: "I find out what kinds of people buy the things that are advertised."
B. communication utility	Motivation to watch commercials in order to provide a basis for later interpersonal communication	4-point agree-disagree items. Scales such as: "I watch commercials to give me something to talk about with my friends."
C. vicarious consumption	Motivation to watch commercials in order to identify with or vicariously participate in attractive life styles	4-point agree-disagree items. Scales such as: "Some of the people they show are examples of what I wish I were."
Attitudes toward TV advertising	Cognitive and effective orientations concerning liking of and belief in TV advertising; advertising as indication of product quality; efficacy of advertising	4-point frequency and "agree-disagree" items, such as: "TV commercials tell the truth"; "TV advertising makes people buy things they don't really want."
Materialism	Orientation emphasizing possessions and money for personal happiness and social progress	4-point frequency and "agree-disagree" items, such as, "It's really true that money can buy happiness."
Advertising recall	Aided recall of national TV advertising campaigns aired during 1969-1970	16 incomplete slogans or descriptions of commercials, such as: "Fly the Friendly Skies of ______."
Effects on buying	Self-reported influence of commercials on purchase behavior; single effect of commercial, or effect of commercial for product already known about	Open-end response to "Did you ever buy a product after seeing it advertised on TV?"

REFERENCES

BAUER, R. A. (1963) "The initiative of the audience." J. of Advertising Research 3: 2-7.

--- and S. GREYSER (1968) Advertising in America: The Consumer View. Boston: Harvard Business School, Division of Research.

CATEORA, P. R. (1963) "An analysis of the teen-age market." Austin: University of Texas Bureau of Business Research.

CHAFFEE, S. and J. McLEOD (1967) "Communication as coorientation: two studies." Presented to the Theory and Methodology Division of the Association for Education in Journalism, Boulder, Colorado.

CHAFFEE, S., S. WARD and L. TIPTON (1967) "Political socialization via mass communication in the 1968 campaign." Presented to the Theory and Methodology Division of the Association for Education in Journalism, Boulder, Colorado.

GRANBOIS, D. H. (1967) "The role of communication in the family decision-making process." Unpublished.

GREENBERG, B. and J. R. DOMINICK (1968) "Television usage, attitudes and functions for low-income and middle-class teenagers." Michigan State University Department of Communication. Unpublished.

HERRMANN, R. O. (1969) The Consumer Behavior of Children and Teenagers: An Annotated Bibliography. Chicago: American Marketing Association.

HESS, R. and J. TORNEY (1967) The Development of Political Attitudes in Children. Chicago: Aldine.

JENNINGS, M. K. and R. C. NIEMI (1968) "Patterns of political learning." Harvard Educational Rev. 38: 443-467.

KENKEL, W. F. (1961) "Family interaction in decision-making on spending," in N. Foote (ed.) Household Decision-Making. Volume 4. New York: New York Univ. Press.

KLAPPER, J. T. (1960) The Effects of Mass Communication. New York: Free Press.

KOMAROVSKY, M. (1961) "Class differences in family decision-making on expenditures," in N. Foote (ed.) Household Decision-Making. Volume 4. New York: New York Univ. Press.

McNEAL, J. U. (1964) "Children as consumers." Marketing Study Series 9. Austin: University of Texas Bureau of Business Research.

OGILVY, D. (1963) Confessions of an Advertising Man. New York: Dell.

PHELAN, G. K. and J. D. SCHVANEVELDT (1969) "Spending and saving patterns of adolescent siblings." J. of Home Economics 61 (February).

POLLAY, R. W. (1969) "A model of family decision-making." Forthcoming.

ROBINSON, J., R. ATHANASIOU, and K. HEAD (1969) Measures of Occupational Attitudes and Occupational Characteristics. Ann Arbor: Survey Research Center.

SCHRAMM, W., J. LYLE, and W. PARKER (1961) Television in the Lives of Our Children. Palo Alto: Stanford Univ. Press.

STEINER, G. (1963) The People Look at Television. New York: Alfred Knopf.

WARD, S. and D. GIBSON (1969) "Social influences and consumer uses of information." Presented to the Advertising Division of the Association for Education in Journalism, Berkeley, California.

WARD, S. and T. ROBERTSON (1970) "Family influence on adolescent consumer behavior." Presented to the American Psychological Association, Miami, Florida.

WELLS, W. (1966) "Children as consumers," in J. Newman (ed.) On Knowing the Consumer. New York: John Wiley.

——— (1965) "Communicating with children." J. of Advertising Research 5, 2: 2-15.

WOLGAST, E. H. (1958) "Do husbands or wives make the purchasing decision?" J. of Marketing 22: 151-158.

The Authors

F. GERALD KLINE is an Associate Professor in the Department of Journalism at the University of Michigan. He has served as Director of Research in the School of Journalism and Mass Communication at the University of Minnesota. His interests center on theory development and methodological advancement as they relate to problems in communication.

PETER CLARKE is Professor of Communication at the University of Michigan. He received his Ph.D. in Communication at the University of Minnesota and has taught there, at the University of Washington and at Wisconsin. His major research interests include the socialization of children's media behavior and information-seeking.

STEVEN H. CHAFFEE and **JACK M. McLEOD** are Professors in the School of Journalism and Mass Communication at the University of Wisconsin (Madison). They are also conducting research applying cognitive and coorientational theories to interpersonal and mass communication, and have studied professional communicators and the effects of mass media campaigns. **CHARLES K. ATKIN** is an Assistant Professor at Michigan State University.

SERENA E. WADE is an Associate Professor in the Department of Speech-Communication at San Jose State College. Prior to joining that faculty she was a member of the Stanford Institute for Communication Research.

PAUL M. HIRSCH is an Assistant Professor at the University of Chicago. His research interests span mass communication and general sociology as well as complex organizations, and he has published other papers dealing with popular music.

RICHARD R. COLE is an Assistant Professor at the University of North Carolina. He has published in *Journalism Quarterly* on "Teenagers and Viewing TV Violence."

ROGER L. BROWN majored in English at the University of Cambridge before proceeding to graduate studies in journalism and communication at the University of Illinois. He was on the staff of the Institute of Communication Research there for a year before returning to England, where he has been a Research Assistant with the Television Research Committee, and is now a Research Officer with the Centre for Mass Communication Research, University of Leicester. Dr. Brown passed away recently. **MICHAEL O'LEARY** was a Research Assistant in the Mass Communication Research Centre at the University of Leicester while this project was underway.

SCOTT WARD is an Associate Professor in the Graduate School of Business Administration, Harvard University, and a Senior Research Associate at the Marketing Science Institute. **DANIEL WACKMAN** is an Associate Professor in the School of Journalism and Mass Communication at the University of Minnesota.